101 Wildflowers of the Ridges Sanctuary

A Field Guide for the Curious

Frances M. Burton and Aurelia M. Stampp

*Photographs by Paul Burton, Bill May,
Paul Regnier, and Janice Stiefel*

Introduction by Paul Regnier

The Ridges Sanctuary
Baileys Harbor, Wisconsin

101 Wildflowers of the Ridges Sanctuary
A Field Guide for the Curious

Frances M. Burton and Aurelia M. Stampp

Published by the Ridges Sanctuary
P.O. Box 152
Baileys Harbor, Wisconsin 54202

Designed by Jane Tenenbaum

Copyright © 2003 Frances M. Burton and Aurelia M. Stampp

ISBN: 0-9726489-0-9
Printed in China

Front cover photo: Gaywings, by Paul Burton
Back cover photo: Bearberry, by Bill May

All proceeds benefit the Ridges Sanctuary

Contents

Map of Door County   v
What Is the Ridges Sanctuary?   vii
Botanical Diagrams   x
Why Write This Book?   xi

The Wildflowers   1

Acknowledgments   99
Sources of Quotes   100
Photo Credits   101
Bibliography   103
Index   107
Checklist of Wildflowers   111

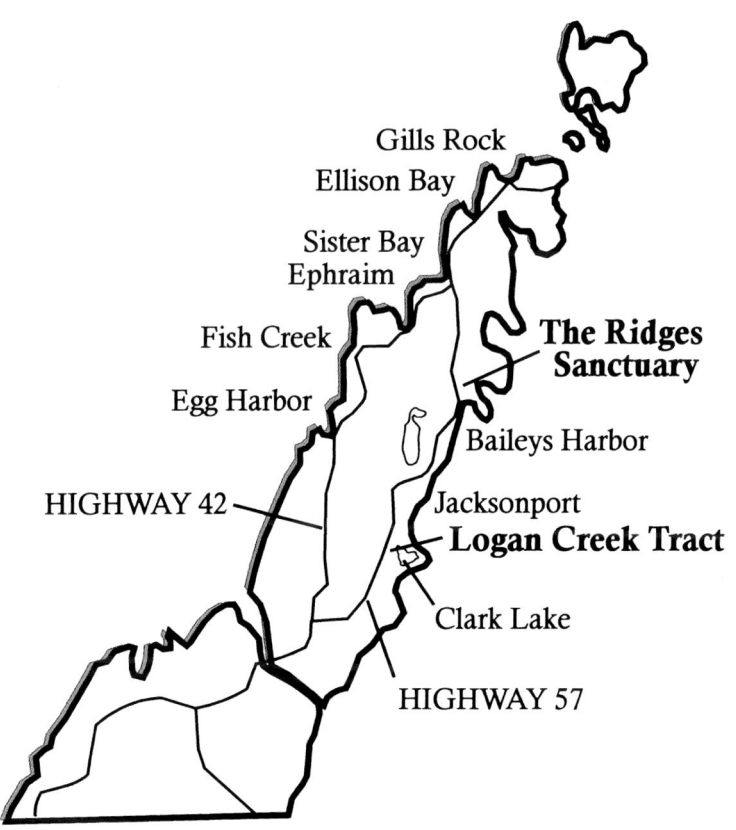

DOOR COUNTY, WISCONSIN

Aerial view of the Ridges Sanctuary showing ridges and swales.
Baileys Harbor Bay is on the right.

What Is the Ridges Sanctuary?
by Paul Regnier, Director

Native wildflowers are perhaps the most significant natural feature of the Ridges Sanctuary. Even the first time visitor is taken by the beauty and diversity of its plant life. Each day the ridges and swales of the Sanctuary bring forth richness that calls for attention, understanding—and appreciation.

The ridges, for which the Sanctuary is named, are the result of a major geological event, combined with wave action and the fluctuating water level of Lake Michigan. Ten thousand years ago the last glacier slowly melted and retreated northward. Great quantities of sand washed out with the melt-water and were deposited in and around the bay that is now known as Baileys Harbor. These sands formed the foundation of a series of parallel, crescent-shaped beach ridges. Sand was, and still is, the basic construction material for beach ridge development. Narrow wetlands known as swales formed between the ridges. Through the combination of incoming sand and lake level changes, a series of thirty or so ridges and swales have been created over the past 1,200 years.

Visitors to the Ridges Sanctuary experience a boreal forest. Boreal forests, more typical of the Far North, are sometimes referred to as northern coniferous forests. They represent the farthest north cover of continuous trees, before giving way to tundra. The dominant tree species are spruce and fir with a sprinkling of alder, aspen, birch, poplar or pine. In the wet or boggy areas, tamarack are common. At the Ridges, where the surrounding dolomitic limestone influences growth conditions, a common species is northern white cedar (arbor vitae).

The boreal forest makes up less than two percent of Wisconsin's vegetative cover. Found only in the extreme northwest corner of the state and along the Lake Michigan shoreline in Door County, these boreal relics persist due to the cooling effect of large bodies of water. The Ridges' boreal forest is thermally buffered by Lake Michigan, which cools it enough to mimic a northern climate.

The boreal forest plant community in the Ridges Sanctuary is not typical of other landscapes located at the 45th parallel in North America. The effects of the local alkaline bedrock, Lake Michigan's moderating influence and moisture, and the dry/wet nature of the ridge and swale complex blend together to create one of the most biologically diverse landscapes in Wisconsin.

Native Americans were the first to live on the sandy ridges—among the spires of balsam fir and white spruce, and perhaps beneath the towering white pines. These early people gathered the seasonal fruit of wild plants like thimbleberry, raspberry, blackberry, cranberry, and blueberries. They used willow shrubs for medicines and collected the resinous sap of the white pine to build or repair their birch bark canoes.

The Baileys Harbor landscape witnessed a dramatic change in the 1800s. The Native Americans were pushed off their lands and early European settlers quickly exploited the rich natural resources. The quiet, lightly inhabited shoreline boomed into an economically important community within a few short years. Once again interest in the Baileys Harbor area focused on plant life—the lumber industry moved in and harvested northern cedars, white pines, tamarack and other native species.

In the 1920s Albert Fuller, Curator of Botany at the Milwaukee Public Museum, traveled the state to gather information for his book on Wisconsin orchids, *Studies of the Flora of Wisconsin Part I: The Orchids*. He was aware of the great diversity of plants, in particular orchids, growing in what is now known as the Ridges Sanctuary and was one of the first to recognize the botanical significance of this ecological treasure.

A few years after Fuller published his book on orchids, he heard that Door County was making plans to develop the area known as "Baileys Harbor Bog" into a trailer park. Truckloads of dolomitic limestone had been dumped into the wet areas to construct a north-south roadway for easier access to the ridges.

With the help of Fuller's information on the value of native plants, especially orchids, concerned citizens in the Baileys Harbor area launched a campaign to preserve the bog. In a February 19, 1937 letter to the *Door County Advocate,* Fuller wrote, "It would be sacrilege …if 'the ridges' area…were to be made into a camp site…The sandy ridges and sloughs provide habitats for more species of plants than any other one locality in Wisconsin…It is almost spectacular that 25 species of orchids should be found in a space less than 40 acres …Surely Door County will not allow any of its natural shrines to be desecrated." Through persistent debate at public meetings, and strong local support, the plans for a trailer park were scrapped and the landscape known as the Ridges Sanctuary was saved from development. On October 4, 1937, ten people signed the Articles of Incorporation for the "Ridges Sanctuary for Plant and Animal Life." Today the original 40 acres have grown to over 1,000 acres.

In the early 1990s, the Ridges expanded its traditional Baileys Harbor boundaries to include a tract of nearly 200 acres of land in the Town of Jacksonport. Characterized by upland beech-maple forest and lowland cedar-dominated woodlands, this tract differs from the ridges and swales of the Baileys Harbor property. Groups of huge hemlock trees create cathedral-like groves in the heavily forested area. Ancient Lake Michigan cobble beaches and wave-cut rocky shores record the lake's early influence on the adjacent land. Over 3,000 feet of shoreline meander along Clark Lake and Logan Creek. For wildflower enthusiasts, the Logan Creek tract is a bonanza of spring ephemerals and early summer flowering plants. The boreal forest of the Ridges and the hardwood forest at Logan Creek are good examples of two major habitats found in Door County.

I hope that you will experience nature in all its grandeur at the Ridges Sanctuary and Logan Creek. These lands reflect the efforts of thousands of people—the Ridges membership—to preserve ecologically significant landscapes for future generations.

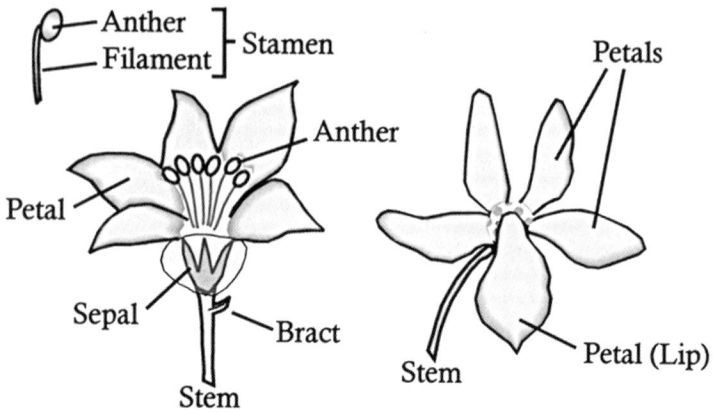

Regular Flower **Irregular Flower**

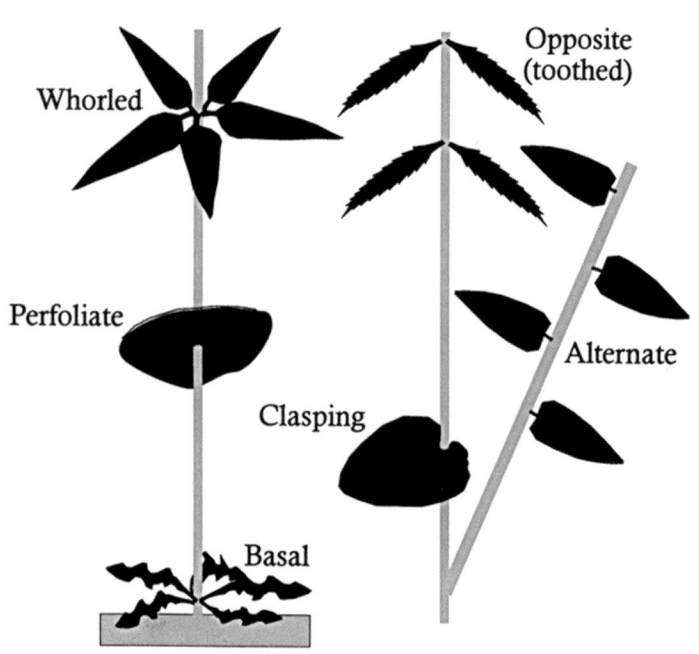

Leaf Arrangements

Why Write This Book?

Finally—a book describing the wildflowers of the Ridges Sanctuary. Founded in 1937, the Ridges is one of the most biologically diverse areas in the state of Wisconsin, but until now there hasn't been a book on its wildflowers. The 101 wildflowers in this book are just a sampling of the more than 500 vascular plants that grow on the Ridges' properties. We chose these particular flowers for a variety of reasons. The majority are the plants most likely to be seen when walking through the Sanctuary or at Logan Creek. However, unusual plants of special interest and beauty are included as well. Some are rare. A few are threatened. All but three are native. The three non-native species included in the book are ones that we consider to be of particular interest.

With a little knowledge, wildflowers can be appreciated and enjoyed for more than just their beauty. Over thousands of years, they have brought pleasure, saved lives, and provided sustenance. They are associated with romance and legends. Like people, they have histories.

Who Is the Intended Reader?

The book presents a simple way to identify and enjoy wildflowers. It's not designed as a botanical text. It's meant to be as comprehensible as possible to the average reader, therefore we used a limited number of botanical terms. For instance, instead of differentiating between "stem" and "stalk," we use "stem" throughout. All the terms we use are illustrated in the drawings on the facing page. The book is meant to be a casual companion—fun, yet informative. There are many fine field guides available that contain precise and detailed botanical information, and we urge anyone interested in wildflowers to consult them as well.

How To Use This Book

The flowers are arranged according to their approximate bloom periods, beginning with the earliest spring flowers. A graph at the bottom of each page shows the range of the bloom period, but growing conditions can cause variation.

Each wildflower is identified first by its common name. Nearly every flower has multiple common names, many of them regional, and we selected those used locally. The scientific name follows in italics. We used the University of Wisconsin Herbarium as our authority for current scientific names. For translations of the scientific names, which are most often in Latin or Greek, we relied on *Gray's Manual of Botany* and Jaeger's *Source-Book of Biological Names and Terms.*

Basic information for identification is listed alongside each flower's photograph. The habitat described is that of the Ridges Sanctuary or Logan Creek, but most of the flowers grow in various places throughout Door County.

A few wildflower species are labeled "Threatened" or "Special Concern." These are designations of the Wisconsin Department of Natural Resources. For more information, see page 16.

How Not To Use This Book

We have reported historical uses of wildflowers (their blossoms, berries, leaves, and roots) as food sources and medicines, but we advocate none of them. The uses are informational only. We strongly advise against using any of the plants medicinally or for consumption. And don't forget, all plants on Ridges property are protected. Picking is strictly prohibited.

The Best Way To Enjoy The Ridges Sanctuary

Remember that "You're only here for a short visit. Don't hurry. Don't worry. And be sure to smell the flowers along the way." (Walter Hagen, 1892–1969, professional golfer)

Frances Burton
Aurelia Stampp
December, 2002

The Wildflowers

Trailing Arbutus
Epigaea repens

ALSO CALLED
  Mayflower
FAMILY Heath
  (Ericaceae)
ORIGIN Native
HEIGHT Creeper
FLOWER White
  tinged with pink,
  in clusters,
  fragrant
LEAF Oval, leathery,
  evergreen
HABITAT Shrubby and
  shady ridges.
Perennial. Grows in the Ridges Sanctuary.

"Arbutus" comes from the Latin word for "strawberry tree." Why the plant received this name is unclear, because it is neither a strawberry nor a tree. *Epigaea* is composed of two Greek words, *epi* meaning "upon" and *gaea* meaning "earth." *Repens* is Latin for "creeping," a name that aptly describes this low-growing plant.

Trailing Arbutus is often the first flower to bloom each spring. The small, ground-hugging plant can be difficult to find, however, because it hides under leaves that protect it from the elements. Although the sturdy, waxy blossoms resist late frosts and cold rains, the plant is sensitive to environmental disturbances and is difficult to transplant. At one time, Trailing Arbutus was so plentiful it was sold in bouquets on the streets of New England towns, but today it is on the rare plant lists of many states.

Native Americans used the fragrant flowers as a skin freshener, and early colonists used the leaves to make a diuretic tea. Legend holds that Trailing Arbutus was the first flower seen by the Pilgrims, who named it after their ship—the Mayflower. But it is also possible the name originated from the time of the year the plant blooms.

Sharp-Lobed Hepatica
Anemone acutiloba

ALSO CALLED Liverleaf
FAMILY Buttercup (Ranunculaceae)
ORIGIN Native
HEIGHT 3–6"
FLOWER Blue, pink, or white
LEAF Basal, 3-lobed
HABITAT Rich deciduous woods. Perennial. Grows at Logan Creek.

Hepatica is a Greek word that means "affecting the liver." The plant received this name because the shape of its leaves resembles the three lobes of the human liver. *Anemone* is from the Greek word *animos* meaning "wind," a name given to a number of wispy-stemmed flowers that tremble in the wind. *Acutiloba* is Latin for "sharp lobe," referring to the pointed leaves.

Early each spring, colonies of Sharp-Lobed Hepatica bloom throughout the Logan Creek woods. Their pale blossoms push through dead leaves, at times before the snow has melted. The mottled purple-brown leaves remain on the plants all winter and are not replaced by fresh green ones until after the flower has bloomed.

The Doctrine of Signatures (see page 12) held that hepatica's liver-shaped leaves were useful in treating liver ailments. That theory was disproved but for a time the plant was used to treat other ailments. Today herbalists say its only use is to ease coughs.

Round-Lobed Hepatica *(Anemone americana)* is nearly identical to Sharp-Lobed Hepatica, but its leaves are rounded rather than pointed, and it prefers a moist, acidic soil.

✤ **CURIOSITY** *The once-popular laxative Sal Hepatica did not use the plant as an ingredient—only its name.*

Apr | May | Jun | Jul | Aug | Sep | Oct

Bloodroot
Sanguinaria canadensis

ALSO CALLED Red Indian Paint
FAMILY Poppy (Papaveraceae)
ORIGIN Native
HEIGHT Up to 12"
FLOWER Large, white with gold center, 8–12 petals
LEAF Scalloped, heavily veined
HABITAT Rich moist woods. Perennial. Grows at Logan Creek.

"Bloodroot" describes the vivid red-orange sap that oozes out when the plant's stem or root is cut. *Sanguinaria* is the Latin word for "blood," and *canadensis* means "of Canada."

Because Bloodroot blooms early in the spring when night temperatures are cool, its leaves remain curled around its stem to conserve warmth. They uncurl after the flower is open and pollination has occurred. Like all plants in the Poppy Family, the flowers are short lived, often lasting only a day or two.

Native Americans used sap from the stem as a topical insect repellent and as a treatment for various skin disorders, such as warts, ringworm, and fungus infections. Although the rhizome is poisonous and internal use was considered dangerous, pioneers used a drop of sap on a lump of maple sugar as a cough medicine and reportedly used dried rhizomes for treating rattlesnake bites.

Bloodroot sap has a long history as a coloring agent. Native Americans used it extensively for war paint and as a dye for fabrics. Early settlers also used it as a red dye, adding oak bark to set the color.

CURIOSITY *In the 1980s, an extract of Bloodroot was used as a plaque-fighting component of Viadent toothpaste and mouthwash.*

Marsh Marigold
Caltha palustris

ALSO CALLED Cowslip, Crazy Bets
FAMILY Buttercup (Ranunculaceae)
ORIGIN Native
HEIGHT 1–2'
FLOWER Yellow, shiny, petal-like sepals
LEAF Basal, heart-shaped
HABITAT Swales, wet meadows, along streams. Perennial. Grows in the Ridges Sanctuary and at Logan Creek.

Marsh Marigold has acquired many common names and nicknames over the years. The name, Marigold, is believed to refer to the flower's use during medieval festivals dedicated to the Virgin Mary. *Caltha* is Greek for "goblet," describing the shape of the flowers, and *palustris* is Latin for "marshy." The name, Cowslip, originated years ago in England where farmers often grazed their cattle on soil too wet to cultivate but not too wet for moisture-loving Marsh Marigolds. Another explanation for "Cowslip" may be the Old English word, *cusluyppe*, meaning "cow slop." The name, Crazy Bets, originated in England where children believed that staring at the flowers would make them crazy.

Marsh Marigolds are one of the few wildflowers that can grow in the middle of a stream, and at times they bloom so profusely the stream has a yellow glow. Many spring butterflies visit the flowers, and during late spring migration, warblers feed on the insects the flowers attract.

Early herbalists used the plant to treat anemia, convulsions, and coughing. Native Americans believed it cured colds and female complaints. Juice, squeezed from the leaves or stem, was applied to warts until they disappeared.

Marsh Marigolds should never be eaten raw. The plant contains toxic glycosides that are rendered harmless only upon cooking. The unopened flower buds can be boiled, pickled, and used like capers. The blossoms can be used to make wine, and they were once a source of yellow dye.

🌿 **CURIOSITY** *Centuries ago English peasants placed Marsh Marigolds on doorsteps of cottages and farmhouses and braided them into garlands as part of May Day festivals.*

Lyre-Leaved Rock Cress
Arabis lyrata

ALSO CALLED Sand Cress
FAMILY Mustard (Brassicaceae)
ORIGIN Native
HEIGHT 4–16"
FLOWER Small, white, in terminal cluster
LEAF Basal, deeply lobed, in rosette
HABITAT Open ridges, trail edges. Perennial/ biennial. Grows in the Ridges Sanctuary.

Arabis is Greek for "Arabia," named by Linnaeus (see page 47) for reasons that are unclear. *Lyrata* means "lyre-shaped," referring to the leaves.

Although some sources say Lyre-Leaved Rock Cress is uncommon due to loss of habitat, it is common in the Ridges Sanctuary. With a bloom period of April to early October, it is one of the Sanctuary's longest flowering plants.

Canada Buffaloberry
Shepherdia canadensis

ALSO CALLED Soapberry, Rabbitberry
FAMILY Oleaster (Elaeagnaceae)
ORIGIN Native
HEIGHT Shrub, 3–7'
FLOWER Very small, yellowish
FRUIT Tiny russet berries
LEAF Silvery-green upper side, rusty spots underside, sparse
HABITAT Shrubby and open ridges, sandy soil. Perennial. Grows in the Ridges Sanctuary.

Native Americans reportedly ate the plant's berries with buffalo meat, thus its common name. *Shepherdia* honors John Shepherd, early nineteenth century botanist and curator of the Liverpool Botanic Gardens. *Canadensis* means "of Canada."

The name, Soapberry, most likely originated in Canada, where the cool-climate shrub is widespread. Although fresh Canada Buffaloberries are too sour to eat without sweetening, indigenous people of British Columbia made "Indian ice cream" by mixing handfuls of the tiny berries with water and sugar, then stirring until the foam resembled soapsuds. Native Americans sometimes preserved the berries or dried them into cakes. Today they are considered too bitter for most tastes, but they can serve as a good source of emergency food.

Trout Lily
Erythronium americanum

ALSO CALLED Fawn Lily
FAMILY Lily (Liliaceae)
ORIGIN Native
HEIGHT 10–12"
FLOWER Yellow, nodding
LEAF Two, heavily mottled
HABITAT Rich, moist woods. Perennial. Grows at Logan Creek.

"Trout" refers to the plant's mottled leaves that some say resemble the coloring of a trout. Others call the plant, Fawn Lily, believing its leaves look like a spotted fawn. *Erythronium* is derived from a Greek word meaning "red," referring to the reddish-brown spots on the leaves. The meaning of *americanum* is obvious.

Although Trout Lily is abundant at Logan Creek, it takes seven years before the plant bears its first blossom. For the first six years, it puts out only one leaf while it stores food in its bulb. By the seventh year, it has finally stored enough food to put out two leaves—and a flower. The flower's curving, petal-like sepals sometimes look wilted because they close in the late afternoon and don't reopen until morning.

Roman soldiers grew Trout Lilies near their camps and used the leaves as poultices to treat foot sores and corns. Native Americans used Trout Lily poultices to draw out splinters and reduce swelling. The leaves are tasty when cooked and eaten with butter, and at one time the small bulbs were stored in root cellars to be used as winter food.

Long-Spurred Violet
Viola rostrata

FAMILY Violet (Violaceae)
ORIGIN Native
HEIGHT 2–8"
FLOWER Lavender-blue, 5 petals, lower petal forms $1/2$" curved spur
LEAF Heart-shaped, toothed
HABITAT Damp Woods. Perennial. Grows at Logan Creek.

SPECIAL CONCERN

Viola is the Latin word for "violet," and *rostrata* means "beaked," referring to the flower's elongated spur.

Long-Spurred Violet is just one of many species of violets that grow at Logan Creek. Violets have five petals: two on the top, one on each side, and a larger one on the bottom. The top and side petals catch the attention of pollinating insects, drawing them to the flower, where the bottom petal functions as a landing pad.

Ancient Greeks used a potion made from violets to induce sleep, strengthen the heart, and calm anger. Romans decorated their banquet tables with thousands of violets in the mistaken belief they could prevent drunkenness. Pliny, an early Roman naturalist, recommended a garland of violets as a cure for hangovers. During the sixteenth century, herbalists prescribed violet potions for a range of complaints that included insomnia, epilepsy, ulcers, and jaundice. In early American medicine, dried plants were used to treat skin and lung diseases, dysentery, ulcers, and cancer. Violets contain salicin (which has an effect similar to its close relative, aspirin) and have been used as pain relievers.

Colorful legends surrounding violets are part of history. Shakespeare was so fond of violets that he often included them in his love sonnets. Napoleon loved violets and kept bouquets of them on his desk.

Violet leaves, high in vitamins A and C, are good in salads or cooked as greens. Added to soup they serve as a thickener, and when dried, they can be made into a tea. The flowers are often candied. In the south of France, violets are cultivated for their oil, which is used in flavoring and to make perfumes.

Pussytoes
Antennaria neglecta

ALSO CALLED Field Pussytoes
FAMILY Daisy (Asteraceae)
ORIGIN Native
HEIGHT 4–16"
FLOWER White, wooly, in tight clusters
LEAF Slender, wooly
HABITAT Fields, banks. Perennial. Grows in the Ridges Sanctuary and at Logan Creek.

Pussytoes received its name because the flower cluster looks like a kitten's paw. *Antennaria* is Latin for "a feeler," because the projected parts of the flower heads of some species look somewhat like insect antennae, and *neglecta* means "overlooked."

Pussytoes' white flower head often appears gray due to its dense covering of hair. The plant seldom grows in the company of other flowers because it gives off a growth-inhibiting substance that poisons the soil for most other plants.

Native Americans chewed stems of the plant as we chew gum today. Appalachian mountain people made a shampoo from the flower heads to eliminate head lice and used dried flower heads as a moth repellent.

Spring Beauty
Claytonia virginica

ALSO CALLED Fairy Spuds
FAMILY Purslane (Portulacaceae)
ORIGIN Native
HEIGHT 6–10"
FLOWER Small, pink with darker pink stripes
LEAF Slender, single pair midway up stem
HABITAT Rich, moist woods. Perennial. Grows at Logan Creek.

Anyone who has seen hundreds of Spring Beauties blooming in the month of May would agree they are appropriately named. *Claytonia* and *virginica* honor John Clayton, a botanist who moved to Virginia from London in the early 1700s.

Spring Beauties carpet the forest floor at Logan Creek. Each dainty flower lasts only two or three days, closing at night or during cloudy weather. Pink veins on the petals act as runways to guide insects to the nectar. Deer browse on the plant's foliage, and chipmunks and mice eat its tubers.

> **FLOWER FACT**
> **Early Blooming Plants**
> It takes energy and food for a plant to produce a flower. Most plants that bloom in early spring depend on food they have produced and stored in their thick roots or bulbs during the preceding growing season. By contrast, plants that bloom in the summer rely on food produced during the current growing season.

Native Americans and early pioneers dug the tiny potato-like tubers and ate them raw, boiled, or baked. Euell Gibbons, well-known plant forager, named them Fairy Spuds. The fresh leaves also are edible and can be added to salads. Spring Beauty is a delicate plant, however, and digging the bulbs or picking the blossoms threatens its existence.

Broad-Leaved Toothwort
Cardamine diphylla

ALSO CALLED Crinkle Root, Pepper Root, Wild Horseradish
FAMILY Mustard (Brassicaceae)
ORIGIN Native
HEIGHT 8–15"
FLOWER White or pale pink, 4 petals, in loose clusters
LEAF Two, each divided into three lobes, toothed
HABITAT Rich open woods. Perennial. Grows at Logan Creek.

Tooth-like projections on its white tubers give the plant its common name. *Cardamine* means "heart-strengthening," because some members of the genus were once used as heart medicines, and *diphylla* means "two leaves."

Patches of Broad-Leaved Toothwort grow along the trails at Logan Creek in spring, but by mid-summer they have died, and all visible traces of the plant have disappeared.

According to the Doctrine of Signatures (see page 12), toothwort cured toothaches, but there is no evidence that it did. The peppery-tasting root is far more useful as a food than a medicine. The raw root tastes like horseradish when chopped and mixed with vinegar and a little salt. Freshly dug roots have a pungent taste, but when dried they become sweet and wrinkle like a prune.

Cut-Leaved Toothwort (*Cardamine concatenata*) grows under the same conditions as Broad-Leaved Toothwort and has the same uses. It, too, is known as Crinkle Root, Pepper Root and Wild Horseradish. Cut-Leaved Toothwort's leaves are deeply cleft, giving rise to its common name, Crow's Toes.

Bellwort
Uvularia grandiflora

ALSO CALLED Perfoliate Bellwort
FAMILY Lily (Liliaceae)
ORIGIN Native
HEIGHT 1–2'
FLOWER Yellow, bell-shaped, drooping
LEAF Downy underside, flower stem appears to grow through leaf (perfoliate)
HABITAT Moist woods. Perennial. Grows at Logan Creek.

The "bell" in Bellwort describes the shape of the blossom, and "wort" is a name formerly given to plants used for food or medicine. *Uvularia* refers to the drooping blossoms said to resemble the uvula, the flap of tissue hanging at the back of the human throat. *Grandiflora* means "large flowers."

In mid-to-late spring, golden-yellow Bellworts welcome visitors to Logan Creek. Even in full bloom, the lovely flowers appear closed and the leaves look droopy and wilted. When the bloom period is over, the stem continues to grow and the leaves no longer droop.

Because Bellwort resembles the uvula, the Doctrine of Signatures held that it was a cure for throat problems, but it was more often used as a poultice to treat wounds and skin inflammations. It has also been used as a food source. Early settlers cooked and ate the young shoots, which taste somewhat like asparagus.

FLOWER FACT
Doctrine of Signatures
The Doctrine of Signatures is an ancient belief that God marked plants and all things in the natural world with signs (signatures) to show their purpose. Distinctive characteristics of a plant determined its healing properties. Examples, in addition to Bellwort, are Bloodroot's red sap, Hepatica's liver-shaped leaves, and Self-Heal's throat-shaped flowers. The Doctrine was codified in the first half of the sixteenth century by its most famous advocate, Paracelsus.

Dutchman's Breeches
Dicentra cucullaria

ALSO CALLED Staggerweed
FAMILY Fumitory (Fumariaceae)
ORIGIN Native
HEIGHT 4–12"
FLOWER White, pantaloon-shaped
LEAF Basal, feathery leaflets
HABITAT Rich woods. Perennial.
  Grows at Logan Creek.

The distinctive blossom of Dutchman's Breeches resembles an upside down pair of yellow-belted Dutch pantaloons hung on a line to dry. *Dicentra* is Greek for "two-spurred," referring to the two legs of the breeches. *Cucullaria* is Latin for "hooded," referring to the two inner petals.

The dangling, white flowers of Dutchman's Breeches arch above its finely divided, grayish-green leaves. Its fragrant blossoms attract Copper, Blue, and Sulphur Butterflies.

Early pioneers used Dutchman's Breeches as a poultice for skin diseases, but the roots contain a hallucinogen, and the plant is mildly poisonous when eaten. Cattle that eat the plant and its attached roots exhibit symptoms that may explain the common name, Staggerweed.

Squirrel Corn *(Dicentra canadensis)* looks similar to Dutchman's Breeches, but its flowers are heart-shaped and fragrant. Its roundish, yellow-orange tubers resemble grains of corn and are eaten by squirrels, thus the name, Squirrel Corn.

Wood Anemone
Anemone quinquefolia

ALSO CALLED Wind Flower
FAMILY Buttercup (Ranunculaceae)
ORIGIN Native
HEIGHT 4–8"
FLOWER White, 4–9 petal-like sepals
LEAF Whorl of three deeply cut leaves
HABITAT Open woods and clearings, often in colonies. Perennial. Grows at Logan Creek.

Anemone comes from the Greek word for "wind," referring to the way the delicate leaves and slender stems tremble in the wind. *Quinquefolia* derives from Latin words meaning "five-leaved," describing the appearance of the leaves.

Because Wood Anemone blooms in early spring when few insects are present, it uses the wind for pollination. With no need to attract insects, it has no nectar and little scent. Like many other early blooming flowers, its seeds are dispersed by ants.

During the Civil War, a surgeon in the Confederate Army used Wood Anemone to remove corns, but cautioned that it was acrid and if used internally could cause a fierce stomachache. Native Americans, however, used a root tea made from Wood Anemone to treat headache, dizziness, and crossed-eyes.

Ancient Romans chanted a prayer while picking the first anemones in spring, asking the gods to safeguard them against disease. But in the Near East, anemones were associated with sickness, and to protect their health, people held their breath and ran past places where anemones were blooming.

FLOWER FACT
Ant Farming

Ant Farming *(Myrmecochory)* describes a symbiotic relationship between ants and certain species of plants, in which the ants help disseminate the plants' seeds. Ants carry seeds to their nests where they eat the seed casings and then discard the seeds in nearby unused tunnels. The seeds germinate and sprout in the tunnels' protected environment.

Big White Trillium
Trillium grandiflorum

ALSO CALLED Wake Robin, Snow Trillium
FAMILY Lily (Liliaceae)
ORIGIN Native
HEIGHT 8–18"
FLOWER Large, white, 3 petals
LEAF Oval, pointed
HABITAT Rich woods. Perennial. Grows in the Ridges Sanctuary and at Logan Creek.

Trillium is derived from a Latin word meaning "sets of three." The plant has three leaves, three petals, three sepals, three stigmas, and six stamens. *Grandiflorum* means "large flowered." The name, Wake Robin, may refer to the plant's use as an aphrodisiac, or it may refer to the fact that it blooms in early spring when robins return.

It takes at least six years for a Trillium to progress from seed to flower. In its first year, the seed germinates underground, and in the second year it sends up a shoot. For the next four years, the plant produces leaves and then—at last—a showy white blossom appears. As the blossom ages, it turns pink. Although Trilliums grow in the Ridges Sanctuary, their preferred habitat is the deciduous woods of Logan Creek where they bloom profusely.

Tea made from Trillium roots was once used to alleviate female discomforts and the pain of childbirth. The roots were also used to treat sore joints, toothache, eye inflammation, and open wounds. Native Americans chewed the roots to ward off the effects of snakebite.

✾ CURIOSITY *Appalachian mountain people believed that picking a Trillium would bring on rain.*

Arctic Primrose
Primula mistassinica

ALSO CALLED Bird's Eye Primrose
FAMILY Primrose (Primulaceae)
ORIGIN Native
HEIGHT 2–8"
FLOWER Pink or lilac, yellow centers
LEAF Basal, hairy underside, toothed
HABITAT Shrubby swales, open ridges near beach. Perennial. Grows in the Ridges Sanctuary.

SPECIAL CONCERN

Arctic Primrose is strictly a northern plant—hence its name. It grows in the harsh climates of Alaska and Canada and in chilly regions around the Great Lakes. *Primula* comes from a Latin word meaning "first" and refers to the plant's early bloom period. *Mistassinica* means "of Lake Mistassini," the largest freshwater lake in Quebec where in 1792 French botanist and explorer, André Michaux, discovered Arctic Primrose. The plant is sometimes called Bird's Eye Primrose because of the yellow "eye" in the center of the blossom.

Botanists postulate that Arctic Primrose seeds were carried to Wisconsin thousands of years ago with the advance of the Canadian ice sheets. The plant continues to thrive in the Ridges Sanctuary where the cooling effect of Lake Michigan helps sustain a boreal forest environment typical of Canada.

FLOWER FACT
Plants in Trouble

According to the Wisconsin Department of Natural Resources, plants in trouble are classified as follows:

- ❧ Endangered: continued existence in Wisconsin is in jeopardy.
- ❧ Threatened: appears likely, within the foreseeable future, to become endangered.
- ❧ Special Concern: species for which some problem of abundance or distribution is suspected but not yet proven.

Dwarf Lake Iris
Iris lacustris

FAMILY Iris (Iridaceae)
ORIGIN Native
HEIGHT 2–4"
FLOWER Bluish-purple, 3 petals with notched tips, 3 sepals with yellow crests
LEAF Lance-shaped, flat
HABITAT Openings on shaded ridges. Perennial. Grows in the Ridges Sanctuary.

THREATENED

For the derivation of *Iris*, see Blue Flag (page 54). *Lacustris* is a Latin word for "of the lake."

This diminutive iris grows near the northern shores of the Great Lakes where it thrives in the cool lake air. Although abundant in the Ridges Sanctuary, Dwarf Lake Iris is considered a rare plant because it requires just the right mix of light, humidity, soil, moisture, and temperature to survive. It grows in only Michigan and Wisconsin. Within Wisconsin it grows only in Door, Brown, and Milwaukee Counties.

Philadelphia naturalist, Thomas Nuttall, discovered Dwarf Lake Iris on Mackinac Island, Michigan in 1810 while conducting the first scientific excursion through the Straits of Mackinac. Since 1988, Dwarf Lake Iris has been listed by Wisconsin Department of Natural Resources and United States Fish and Wildlife Service as "threatened." Its habitat has been greatly reduced by shoreline development, road widening, chemical spraying, and off-road vehicle use.

Starflower
Trientalis borealis

ALSO CALLED Chick Wintergreen, Maystar
FAMILY Primrose (Primulaceae)
ORIGIN Native
HEIGHT 4–8"
FLOWER White, star-shaped, usually 7 petals
LEAF Pointed, 5–9 in whorl
HABITAT Shaded ridges, moist woods. Perennial. Grows in the Ridges Sanctuary and at Logan Creek.

Even the casual observer can understand how Starflower received its common name. *Trientalis* comes from a Latin word meaning "third part of a foot," referring to the diminutive plant's height, and *borealis* means "northern," referring to its northern growing range.

In the Ridges Sanctuary, Starflower often blooms in company with Dwarf Lake Iris and Gaywings, forming a broad, multi-colored carpet. Few plant species have flower parts in multiples of seven, but Starflower, in addition to having seven petals, has seven yellow stamens.

Chick Wintergreen is another common name for Starflower. The reasons are unclear, as Susan Cooper (James Fenimore Cooper's daughter) pointed out. "Some persons call this chick wintergreen, a name which is an insult to the plant, and to the common sense of the community. Why, it is one of the daintiest wood flowers, with nothing in the world to do with chicks, or weeds, or winter. It is not the least of an evergreen, its leaves withering in autumn, as a matter of course, and there is not a chicken in the country that knows it by sight or taste. Discriminating people, when they first find its elegant silvery flower growing in the woods beside the violet, call it Maystar."

Gaywings
Polygala paucifolia

ALSO CALLED Fringed Polygala
FAMILY Milkwort (Polygalaceae)
ORIGIN Native
HEIGHT 3–7"
FLOWER Bright magenta, irregular, fringed
LEAF Oval, clustered at top of stem, evergreen
HABITAT Shrubby and shaded ridges. Perennial. Grows in the Ridges Sanctuary.

"Gaywings" refers to the plant's two winged sepals. *Polygala* is Greek for "much milk," stemming from the belief that plants of the Milkwort Family increased milk production in nursing mothers and cows. *Paucifolia* is Latin for "few-leaved."

This delightful little wildflower looks like a miniature airplane. Susan Fenimore Cooper thought the flowers looked like butterflies and described them as "…growing low as they do and many of their winged flowers together, you might fancy them so many warm lilac, or deep rose-colored butterflies resting on the moss."

CURIOSITY *Because of its bilateral symmetry and intense color, many visitors to the Ridges mistakenly think this showy little flower is an orchid—but it's not. It's a member of the Milkwort Family.*

FLOWER FACT
Three Good Reasons to Not Pick Wildflowers

- It diminishes a plant's chances of reproducing by limiting the number of seeds it can produce.
- It may be against the law—unless the plant is on your property.
- Imagine what would happen if each of the Ridges 20,000 annual visitors picked just one flower!

Bearberry
Arctostaphylos uva-ursi

ALSO CALLED Kinnikinnick
FAMILY Heath (Ericaceae)
ORIGIN Native
HEIGHT Low, shrub-like
FLOWER White or pale pink, nodding, urn-shaped
FRUIT Red
LEAF Thick, shiny, evergreen
HABITAT Open and shrubby ridges. Perennial. Grows in the Ridges Sanctuary.

Arctostaphylos is from two Greek words meaning "bear" and "bunch of grapes." *Uva-ursi* means "bear's grapes" in Latin. Both *Arctostaphylos* and *uva-ursi* refer to the fruit, presumably a favorite of bears. "Kinnikinnick," in the Algonquin language, refers to any leaf that could be smoked, as in a pipe.

Over the years, herbalist-physicians have put Bearberry to a remarkable number of uses. They used it as an astringent, emetic, cathartic purge, and blood purifier—as well as to treat uterine hemorrhages, catarrh, and chronic bronchitis. In 1798 a physician and professor of botany at the University of Pennsylvania claimed that Bearberry "should be in the hands of every physician."

The dried leaves make a tobacco substitute. Prince Maximillian of Prussia, explorer and naturalist, spent the winter of 1833 with Native Americans in what is now North Dakota. He wrote, "When the Blackfeet smoke…their tobacco consists of the small, roundish, dried leaves of the sakakomi plant *Arctostaphylos uva-ursi*. When you visit an Indian in his tent, the pipe is immediately taken up and passes round in the company, each person handing it to his left-hand neighbour. The master of the tent often blows the smoke towards the sun and the earth; everyone takes some puffs and hands it on."

Goldthread
Coptis trifolia

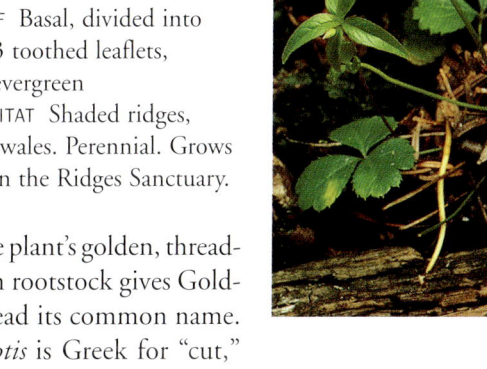

ALSO CALLED Canker Root, Dye Root
FAMILY Buttercup (Ranunculaceae)
ORIGIN Native
HEIGHT 3–6"
FLOWER White, 5–7 petal-like sepals, numerous yellow stamens
LEAF Basal, divided into 3 toothed leaflets, evergreen
HABITAT Shaded ridges, swales. Perennial. Grows in the Ridges Sanctuary.

The plant's golden, thread-thin rootstock gives Goldthread its common name. *Coptis* is Greek for "cut," referring to the divided leaves, and *trifolia* means "three leaves."

Both Native Americans and colonists chewed the bitter root to treat mouth sores, giving rise to the common name, Canker Root. The root contains the alkaloid, berberine (a mild sedative), and even today it is used to sooth teething babies.

The bright yellow roots were at one time highly valued for making dye and were sold commercially until 1908. Native Americans used the roots to dye porcupine quills and feathers.

🌿 CURIOSITY *"It was a woman who discovered the little goldthread— a woman who possibly felt an affinity for bogs and the chill northern forests, for she could have found it nowhere else. Miss Jane Colden collected it in upper New England in 1758. It should more appropriately have been named in her honor… Perhaps there was an aversion to women botanists at that time" (Virginia S. Eifert,* **Journeys in Green Places***).*

Wild Strawberry
Fragaria virginiana

ALSO CALLED Common Strawberry
FAMILY Rose (Rosaceae)
ORIGIN Native
HEIGHT Creeper
FLOWER White, 5 petals
FRUIT Red, seeds on surface
LEAF Oval, toothed, in groups of 3
HABITAT Shrubby ridges, woodland edges. Perennial. Grows in the Ridges Sanctuary.

The fruit of the plant appears scattered or "strewn" among the leaves, which gave rise to the name "strewberry." The plant's name eventually became "strawberry." *Fragaria* is derived from the Latin word for "fragrant," referring to the sweet aroma of the berry. *Virginiana* refers to the state where Wild Strawberry was first described.

Wild Strawberries are rich in vitamins A and C, as well as in iron. Native Americans used strawberry juice mixed with water as a remedy for sore eyes, and herbalists used the roots to treat mouth ulcers, kidney stones, and gonorrhea. Linnaeas (see page 47) maintained that he was cured of gout by eating Wild Strawberries.

Perhaps it was Wild Strawberry jam that inspired Izaak Walton (quoting a Dr. Butler) to write, "Doubtless God could have made a better berry, but doubtless God never did."

🌿 **CURIOSITY** *Cultivated strawberries are hybrids of Wild Strawberries and Beach Strawberries (**Fragaria chiloensis**), the result of an accidental hybridization that took place in Holland in the 1750s.*

Jack-in-the-Pulpit
Arisaema triphyllum

ALSO CALLED Indian Turnip
FAMILY Arum (Araceae)
ORIGIN Native
HEIGHT 1–3'
FLOWER Arching, greenish-purple streaked spathe ("pulpit") encircling an erect spadix ("jack"); spadix bears tiny flowers
FRUIT Dense cluster of red berries
LEAF Divided into three leaflets
HABITAT Damp woods, swamps. Perennial. Grows at Logan Creek.

"Jack" was once a common colloquialism for "fellow." *Arisaema* combines two Greek words that refer to the purple stripes on the pulpit, and *triphyllum* means "three leaves."

Jack-in-the-Pulpit has its own built-in umbrella—the hood over the pulpit protects the flowering jack and prevents the pulpit from filling with water. Tiny flowers at the base of the jack become visible when the pulpit withers away. The flowers later form an eye-catching clump of shiny, scarlet berries.

Early settlers pounded Jack-in-the-Pulpit root into a powder and used it as a poultice for sore eyes, headaches, ringworm, and rattlesnake bites. The Doctrine of Signatures (see page 12) held that the jack was an aphrodisiac.

The plant, root, and berries are not edible raw. They contain calcium oxalate crystals that cause an intense burning sensation in the mouth. Native Americans sometimes used the plant's large root as a rite of passage. Before they could officially enter manhood, young men had to eat a raw root without flinching.

🌿 **CURIOSITY** *Starch from the root was once used for starching shirt ruffs, but laundresses' hands became so irritated that the practice was discontinued.*

Blue Cohosh
Caulophyllum thalictroides

ALSO CALLED Papoose Root
FAMILY Barberry (Berberidaceae)
ORIGIN Native
HEIGHT 1–3'
FLOWER Very small, yellow-green, in clusters
FRUIT Dusty blue
LEAF Large, 3 lobes
HABITAT Rich woods. Perennial. Grows at Logan Creek.

"Blue Cohosh" takes its name from the blue of its fruit and the bluish color of its new leaves. "Cohosh" is an Algonquin Indian word meaning "it is rough," perhaps referring to the rootstock. *Caulophyllum* is from the Greek, *caulos* meaning "stem," and *phyllon* meaning "leaf." *Thalictroides* refers to the resemblance of the leaves to those of Meadow Rue *(Thalictrum dioicum)*.

   Although Blue Cohosh roots are mildly poisonous, when used with caution they have long been known as an excellent medicine. Native Americans called the plant, Papoose Root, and believed a root tea taken a week or so prior to childbirth would facilitate a rapid and painless delivery. Early pioneers used the roots to treat ailments ranging from rheumatism to epilepsy to fever to colic. At one time, pharmacists collected, prepared, and sold the roots and rhizomes for medicinal use. Today Blue Cohosh continues to be used by herbalists. For example, Dr. John Christopher's B&B Tincture, containing Blue Cohosh and four other herbs, is marketed as a remedy for sore throats, hiccups, and nervous conditions.

Indian Paintbrush
Castilleja coccinea

ALSO CALLED Painted Cup
FAMILY Figwort (Scrophulariaceae)
ORIGIN Native
HEIGHT 1–2'
FLOWER Scarlet-tipped bracts surrounding inconspicuous greenish-yellow flowers
LEAF Basal leaves in rosette; stem leaves in narrow segments
HABITAT Open, sunny ridges. Annual/Biennial. Grows in the Ridges Sanctuary.

The red-tipped bracts, often mistaken for flower petals, appear to have been dipped in paint, giving Indian Paintbrush its common name. *Castilleja* honors eighteenth century Spanish botanist, Domingo Castillejo, and *coccinea* means "scarlet."

Indian Paintbrush is a hemiparasitic plant (see page 30). Its roots have the ability to tap into the roots of nearby plants, particularly grasses, and extract water and mineral nutrients.

Native American tribes used various parts of the plant for medicinal purposes. Hopi women used a tea made from the entire plant as a contraceptive, the Chippewa tribe used its leaves to treat rheumatism, and Navajos used a tea made from the blossoms to soothe burned skin and treat centipede bites.

Long ago, according to legend, a young Indian man tried to paint a picture of an evening sunset, using only his war paints. When he failed in his efforts to capture its wonderfully vibrant colors, he turned to the Great Spirit for help. The Great Spirit responded with a gift of paintbrushes dipped in all the colors of the sunset. After the young man used the brushes, he tossed them away. Wherever a brush landed, an Indian Paintbrush plant sprang up.

Canada Mayflower
Maianthemum canadense

ALSO CALLED Wild Lily of the Valley
FAMILY Lily (Liliaceae)
ORIGIN Native
HEIGHT 2–8"
FLOWER Very small, white, star-shaped, in clusters
FRUIT Red
LEAF Lance-shaped, veined
HABITAT Shaded ridges and swales; moist woods. Perennial. Grows in the Ridges Sanctuary and at Logan Creek.

Maianthemum comes from two Greek words, *Maia*, meaning "May" and *anthemon*, meaning "flower." According to legend, the flower was named for Maia, daughter of Atlas and mother of Mercury. She was said to be so beautiful that only an exceptionally lovely flower could be named in her honor. *Canadense* refers to Canada. With its pointed oval leaves and small white flowers, the plant is often referred to as Wild Lily of the Valley.

This common woodland plant spreads by means of a creeping rootstock, frequently forming dense colonies. Canada Mayflower's translucent red berries remain on the plant throughout the winter, providing food for grouse and chipmunks.

Canada Mayflower has few medicinal uses. Although it is reputed to be quite poisonous if eaten raw, Native Americans used tea made from the whole plant to cure headaches. A substitute for digitalis can be made from the root, but it is not in great demand. The ripe berries are very bitter and somewhat cathartic. They can be made into jelly but only with the addition of plenty of sugar!

White Baneberry
Actaea pachypoda

ALSO CALLED Doll's Eyes, Poisonberry
FAMILY Buttercup (Ranunculaceae)
ORIGIN Native
HEIGHT 1–2'
FLOWER Small, white, oblong cluster
FRUIT White with black dot
LEAF Oval, pointed, toothed
HABITAT Rich woods. Perennial. Grows in the Ridges Sanctuary and at Logan Creek.

"Bane," meaning "to cause death," comes from an ancient English word that appears in *Beowulf*. It refers to the plant's poisonous fruit. *Actaea* is a Greek word for the Elder Tree whose leaves are similar to White Baneberry's. *Pachypoda* means "thick footed," referring to the plant's thick stems.

White Baneberry is better known for its fruit than its flowers. The clusters of small, white flowers are easy to overlook, but the eye-catching berries are the origin of the folk name, Doll's Eyes.

Although all baneberry fruit is poisonous, Native Americans used the leaves for a variety of medicinal purposes. Cheyenne women, who often nursed their children until they were three or four years old, drank baneberry tea to increase milk secretion. Other Native Americans used baneberry to wash their babies. The Chippewa believed that White Baneberry cured women's diseases, and Red Baneberry cured men's diseases.

Red Baneberry *(A. rubra)* is nearly identical to White Baneberry except for the color of the berries—a shiny deep red. Red Baneberry favors cooler climates than White Baneberry.

Starry Solomon's Plume
Smilacina stellata

ALSO CALLED Starry False Solomon's Seal
FAMILY Lily (Liliaceae)
ORIGIN Native
HEIGHT 1–2'
FLOWER Small, white, star-shaped, in terminal cluster
FRUIT Small, maroon
LEAF Narrow, on zigzag stem
HABITAT Open ridges. Perennial.
Grows in the Ridges Sanctuary.

It's easy to see why this plant is called "starry"—each flower looks like a tiny six-pointed star. The loose cluster of flowers at the top of the stem gives the appearance of a "plume," but why Solomon? It's a mystery. *Smilacina* is a diminutive of the word "smilax," a similar but unrelated plant, and *stellata* means "starry."

Starry Solomon's Plume's preferred habitat is shaded places, but the widespread plant also grows in thickets, open forests, sandy areas, and meadows. Six tepals (modified petals) and six anther-tipped filaments give the flowers their distinctive, starlike appearance. The

black-striped green berries turn maroon as they mature, and in fall they are a food source for Ruffed Grouse.

The berries are edible but not particularly tasty and may have a laxative effect. The fresh roots are useful as anti-inflammatories and astringents. When chopped and cooked with honey, the roots make a good cough syrup, and the ground root soothes rashes, burns, and insect bites.

Bog Rosemary
Andromeda glaucophylla

FAMILY Heath (Ericaceae)
ORIGIN Native
HEIGHT Shrub up to 2'
FLOWER Small, pinkish, urn-shaped, in tight clusters
LEAF Narrow, white underside, evergreen
HABITAT Open and boggy swales. Perennial. Grows in the Ridges Sanctuary.

"Rosemary" refers to the resemblance of the plant's leaves to those of the herb, rosemary. *Andromeda* is a rather imaginative name given to Bog Rosemary by Linnaeus (see page 47). According to Greek Mythology, Andromeda was a princess of Ethiopia who was chained to a rock in the sea and destined to be eaten by a sea monster. She was dramatically rescued by Perseus, whom she later married. Why Andromeda? Apparently only Linnaeus knew. *Glaucophylla* is Greek for "silvery leaf," referring to the dense white hairs covering the underside of each leaf.

Bog Rosemary's leathery evergreen leaves have an inward-rolled edge much like those of Labrador Tea, a common plant of the Ridges Sanctuary (page 38). The two plants grow in similar environments and can be distinguished by the undersides of their leaves—white for Bog Rosemary and rusty for Labrador Tea. Bog Rosemary needs two full growing seasons to complete its cycle from bud to mature fruit. The first spring it produces leaves, followed by flower buds in early summer. The buds do not open that summer but overwinter and bloom the following year.

Bog Rosemary should not be eaten and is poisonous to livestock. It contains the cardiac glycoside, andromedotoxin, which can cause loss of motor control and hallucinations.

Cancer Root
Orobanche uniflora

SPECIAL CONCERN

ALSO CALLED One-Flowered Broomrape
FAMILY Broomrape (Orobanchaceae)
ORIGIN Native
HEIGHT 3–10"
FLOWER Whitish or pale lavender, yellow center
LEAF Small cream-colored scales at base of stem
HABITAT Damp sandy ridges. Perennial? Annual? (Authorities differ). Grows in the Ridges Sanctuary.

Cancer Root received its name because it is a "cancer" or "growth" on other plants. *Orobanche* is Greek for "vetch strangler," alluding to Cancer Root's parasitism, although the likely host is not a vetch. *Uniflora* means one-flowered.

Cancer Root is parasitic on other plants, so it does not photosynthesize or have green leaves. It is a rare sight to see this lovely but peculiar-looking plant. It may appear in the Ridges Sanctuary one year and not appear again for another five years.

FLOWER FACT Plants That Feed Off Other Plants

Because they obtain their nourishment from other plants, parasitic and saprophytic plants do not require chlorophyll or have green leaves. True parasitic plants, such as Cancer Root and Beechdrops (page 96), feed on other living plants. Saprophytic plants, such as Striped Coralroot (page 39) and Indian Pipe (page 61) also feed on other plants but not on living plants. They derive their nourishment from dead or decaying roots, often in the presence of an intermediate soil fungus that helps break down vegetation. A related type of plant is known as hemiparasitic. These plants are green and contain chlorophyll, but they depend to some extent on other plants for their nutrition. Examples are Indian Paintbrush (page 25) and Bastard Toadflax (page 31).

Bastard Toadflax
Comandra umbellata

ALSO CALLED
  False Toadflax
FAMILY
  Sandalwood (Santalaceae)
ORIGIN Native
HEIGHT 6–16"
FLOWER Small, greenish-white, 5 pointed sepals, in cluster
LEAF Oblong, pale underside
HABITAT Thickets, dry open woods. Perennial. Grows in the Ridges Sanctuary.

The plant's common name is an enigma, because it has nothing to do with toads and it isn't a flax or even a toadflax. "Bastard" means "false" and probably refers to the fact that Bastard Toadflax is not related to true Toadflax *(Linaria)*. *Comandra* comes from two Greek words that roughly translate as "man's hair" and refers to hairs on the anthers (the pollen-bearing part of the stamens). *Umbellata* means "bearing umbels" (an umbel is a "flower cluster in which the flower stalks arise from the same point, like the ribs of an umbrella").

Bastard Toadflax is hemiparasitic (see page 30), meaning it is a photosynthetic plant that produces some of its own food, but it is also parasitic, drawing some of its nutrients from the roots of nearby trees or shrubs. Its small, star-shaped flowers do not have petals but are composed of modified leaves called sepals.

The plant has been used as a leaf tea to treat coughs and breathing difficulties. The immature flowers are said to be an effective cough suppressant when licked like a lozenge.

Buckbean
Menyanthes trifoliata

ALSO CALLED Bogbean
FAMILY Buckbean (Menyanthaceae)
ORIGIN Native
HEIGHT Up to 1'
FLOWER White, bearded inside with white hairs
LEAF Three oval leaflets on stalk arising from rhizome
HABITAT Open swales. Perennial. Grows in the Ridges Sanctuary.

"Buckbean" is a translation of the Dutch word *boksboon*. *Bok* means "buck" or "deer," and *boon* means "bean." "Bean" apparently refers to the resemblance of the plant's leaves to those of garden beans, but the reason for "buck" is unclear. *Menyanthes* derives from two Greek words meaning "disclosing" and "flower," describing the arrangement of the flowers on the stem. *Trifoliata* means "three-leaved."

Growing in water alongside bridges in the Sanctuary, frosty-appearing Buckbean flowers seem to glow. Virginia Eifert, writing about the Ridges in *Journeys in Green Places*, described Buckbean's flowers as "white stars, thickly feathered with upstanding white hairs, accented by purple-black stamens and the gentle pink of the buds."

Buckbean leaves possess strong tonic properties. The finely powdered leaves have been used as remedies for rheumatism, skin diseases, and the once-dreaded scurvy. Warning! The leaves can be a powerful purgative.

The ground roots are extremely bitter, but when thoroughly leached they can be used to make a nourishing but unsavory flour. Laplanders and Finns used the flour to make a type of bread they referred to as "famine bread."

Silverweed
Argentina anserina

ALSO CALLED Crampweed
FAMILY Rose (Rosaceae)
ORIGIN Native
HEIGHT Low, spreading
FLOWER Yellow, 5 petals
LEAF Sharply toothed, silvery underneath, sprouting from runners
HABITAT Shrubby and sandy swales, beaches. Perennial. Grows in the Ridges Sanctuary.

Long silvery hairs on the undersides of its leaves give the plant its common name. *Argente* is a Latin word meaning "silvery." *Anserina* means "of geese." Why *anserina*? No one seems to know.

Silverweed's bright flowers and long, reddish runners make it easy to recognize. Flowers and leaves arise from the runners on separate stems. A single flower tops each long, smooth flower stem, while the erect leaf stem contains numerous leaflets that increase in size from bottom to top

From the time of Hippocrates, Silverweed has been considered a powerful medicine and has been used to treat ailments ranging from fevers and toothaches to ulcers and cancers. It has even been used to remove freckles and pimples. The name, Crampweed, comes from the Shakers who used Silverweed leaf tea to treat diarrhea.

The roots of Silverweed were once an important food source in Britain and Northern Europe. Before the introduction of the potato in Ireland, Silverweed was cultivated for its roots. Native Americans also ate the roots, both raw and cooked. They taste like sweet potatoes or parsnips, and even today, books of edible wild foods list them as a delicious dietary addition.

Sweet Cicely
Osmorhiza claytonii

ALSO CALLED Hairy Sweet Cecily
FAMILY Carrot (Apiaceae)
ORIGIN Native
HEIGHT 1–3'
FLOWER Very small, white, in clusters
FRUIT Blackish-green, fuzzy
LEAF Fernlike
HABITAT Moist, rich deciduous woods. Perennial. Grows at Logan Creek.

Sad to say, Sweet Cicely wasn't a charming young lady with a delightful disposition. Instead, the name is a derivative of the Greek word, *seseli*, meaning "sweet scented plant." *Osmorhiza* comes from two Greek words meaning "scented root." *Claytonii* honors John Clayton, early Virginia botanist.

After early spring flowers have finished blooming, the woods at Logan Creek are filled with Sweet Cicely's leafy foliage and tiny flowers. The plant is best known for the part that doesn't show—the aromatic root. When crushed or chewed, it tastes and smells like licorice or anise. The fruit, too, has a spicy taste. Native Americans used root tea to treat stomach ailments, and before "store-bought" candy was available, mountain folks enjoyed chewing the roots for their sweet, refreshing taste.

FLOWER FACT Folk Remedies

The recorded medicinal use of plants dates back to 1770 B.C., and many of today's drugs contain substances originally found in plants. Until recently, however, herbal medicine was risky business. People relied on trial and error and often the cure was as deadly as the disease. Although herbal remedies are in use today, the uses described in this book should be viewed only as historical folklore—they are not recommendations for treatment.

Bunchberry
Cornus canadensis

ALSO CALLED Dwarf Cornel
FAMILY Dogwood (Cornaceae)
ORIGIN Native
HEIGHT 3–8"
FLOWER Four white petals (bracts)
LEAF Pointed, 4–6, in whorl
FRUIT Shiny, red
HABITAT Shady ridges and swales. Perennial. Grows in the Ridges Sanctuary.

Small bunches of scarlet berries give this plant its common name. *Cornus* is Latin for "antler," referring to the tough woody stems of plants in the Dogwood Family, and *canadensis* means "of Canada."

Bunchberry, smallest member of the Dogwood Family, spreads by underground rhizomes, sometimes forming large patches. The flower's appearance is deceiving. What look like white petals are actually bracts (modified leaves) surrounding a cluster of tiny yellow-green flowers. The flowers become berries that provide food for a variety of birds, including partridge, grouse, veery, and vireo, as well as deer and other denizens of the woods.

Early settlers treated colic in babies with a mild tea brewed from bunchberry roots, and practicing herbalists told their patients to chew bunchberry twigs to prevent fevers.

Bunchberries are tasteless and fairly dry, but after cooking and straining to remove the large pits, they can be mixed with other fruits to make jellies or jams. Laplanders made bunchberry pudding by boiling strained berries with whey. To enhance the flavor, they served the pudding with sugar and cream.

Clintonia
Clintonia borealis

ALSO CALLED Blue Bead Lily
FAMILY Lily (Liliaceae)
ORIGIN Native
HEIGHT 6–16"
FLOWER Greenish-yellow, bell-shaped
FRUIT Shiny, blue
LEAF Basal, large, thick
HABITAT Shady ridges, moist woods. Perennial. Grows in the Ridges Sanctuary.

Clintonia honors New York Governor, De Witt Clinton (1769–1828). Clinton was responsible for the construction of the Erie Canal and was the author of books on natural history. *Borealis* means "of the north."

Clintonia's nodding flower often appears to be beyond its peak when, in fact, it has just started to bloom. The plant is more noted for its clusters of beautiful blue berries than for its flowers.

The young leaves of Clintonia taste and smell like cucumber and are good in salads. Country people in Maine used them extensively as a potherb. The blue berries, though beautiful, are tasteless, thought to be poisonous, and should not be eaten.

FLOWER FACT **The Beauty of Berries**

"Flowers are only one part of the color and texture to be found in forests and fields. As plants mature and bear fruit, the berries and seeds can be just as spectacular with interesting colors, patterns, and shapes" (Susan M. Sander, *Wildflowers, A Guide for Washington Island and Door County*).

Swamp Buttercup
Ranunculus hispidus

ALSO CALLED Hispid Buttercup
FAMILY Buttercup
  (Ranunculaceae)
ORIGIN Native
HEIGHT 1–3'
FLOWER Yellow, glossy, 5 petals, hairy stem
LEAF Deeply cleft, divided into 3 segments
HABITAT Shaded swales. Perennial. Grows in the Ridges Sanctuary.

"Buttercup" originates from the mistaken belief that the flower, if eaten by cows, gave yellow color to butter, but in reality cows avoid the plant. *Ranunculus* is Latin for "small frog," possibly because both frogs and buttercups like moist environments. *Hispidus* means "shaggy" or "rough," referring to the stem.

The distinctive light-reflecting texture of buttercup's petals is caused by a layer of special cells located just below the surface. Light reflected from the glossy, yellow petals attracts pollinating insects.

At one time buttercups were used medically—but the results were often unpleasant. The plant can cause intestinal irritation if eaten and painful skin blisters if handled. Early physicians frequently used buttercups to remove warts and other unwanted growths, and European street beggars rubbed buttercup juice on their skin to cause ulcers, hoping passersby would pity them. Over time doctors substituted less noxious remedies, and today herbalists warn against the use of buttercups.

FLOWER FACT

Plants Can Hurt You!

A great many plants are known for their medicinal qualities, but many others are harmful. For example, Showy Lady's Slipper can cause a nasty skin rash, Death Camas can cause dizziness, slow heart rate and coma, and Bulb-Bearing Water Hemlock can cause death. For your own safety, enjoy the beauty of wildflowers, but leave them untouched.

Labrador Tea
Ledum groenlandicum

ALSO CALLED Hudson's Bay Tea
FAMILY Heath (Ericaceae)
ORIGIN Native
HEIGHT Shrub, up to 3'
FLOWER Small, white, in clusters
LEAF Green above, rusty-orange below
HABITAT Shaded ridges, shrubby swales, margins of open swales. Perennial. Grows in the Ridges Sanctuary.

"Labrador" refers to a large Canadian peninsula near Hudson Bay, where the plant is common. Tea brewed from its fragrant leaves is known as Labrador Tea or Hudson's Bay Tea. *Ledum* refers to an ancient Greek plant whose fragrance was similar to that of Labrador Tea, and *groenlandicum* means "of Greenland."

Labrador Tea is a common sight alongside the bridges and trails in the Ridges Sanctuary. Its distinctive wooly leaves make it easy to identify, even when not in bloom.

Labrador Tea is not technically a "tea," but it is often used to make a beverage. A pleasant drink made from the plant's leaves was popular during the American Revolution. Thoreau remarked that such a drink "has a rather agreeable fragrance, between turpentine and strawberries…and sometimes reminds me of the peculiar scent of a bee." A merchant in the Hudson Bay area once reported that drinking a pint of strong Labrador Tea daily for three months cured him of a nervous disorder, and eccentric botanist, Constantine Rafinesque, claimed that such a brew would kill lice and ticks.

❧ CURIOSITY *The leaves of Labrador Tea are useful in closets to protect against moths.*

Striped Coralroot
Corallorhiza striata

FAMILY Orchid (Orchidaceae)
ORIGIN Native
HEIGHT 8–20"
FLOWER Striped, reddish-pink
LEAF Purplish scales on reddish-pink stem
HABITAT Shaded ridges, rich woods. Perennial. Grows in the Ridges Sanctuary and at Logan Creek.

Its boldly striped petals and pink, coral-like root give this orchid its common and scientific names. *Corallorhiza* means "coral root," referring to the similarity of its root system to that of coral formations—not to the color of its flowers. *Striata* means "striped," referring to the leaves and flowers.

Striped Coralroot, a plant that may grow as a single stem or as a clump, is not always easy to find. Its stems blend into its surroundings, and it has the habit of not reappearing in the same spot each year. The plant can tolerate cold but not heat, and most of its range is in Canada. It apparently survived along the edges of the last glacier and spread northward after the ice melted. Striped Coralroot is a saprophytic plant (see page 30) and contains no chlorophyll or green leaves.

Coralroot was known by herbalists for centuries, but its scarcity and high price precluded widespread use.

Wild Sarsaparilla
Aralia nudicaulis

ALSO CALLED Sassparilla
FAMILY Ginseng (Araliaceae)
ORIGIN Native
HEIGHT 8–18"
FLOWER Very small, greenish-white, in 3 spherical clusters
FRUIT Purple berries
LEAF 3 branching parts, each with 3–5 leaflets
HABITAT Shaded ridges. Perennial. Grows in the Ridges Sanctuary and at Logan Creek.

The word, Sarsaparilla, is Spanish, meaning "a bush" or "a little vine." *Aralia* is derived from the French Canadian name for the plant, and *nudicaulis* means "nude stem," referring to the leafless stem.

Sarsaparilla's small round flower clusters are not eye-catching and can easily be overlooked, but viewed closely, they resemble tiny exploding fireworks. Its leaves are so similar to those of poison ivy that casual hikers often confuse the two.

The plant's root has long been used for both medicine and food. Both Native Americans and early pioneers used it to treat a wide variety of ailments, including syphilis and infected sores.

Sarsaparilla's large fleshy root is nutritious and was used as a food source by Native Americans while on forced marches or long hunting trips. The root has a pleasant aroma and taste, and although it has been used as an ingredient in making root beer, it was not an ingredient in the once-popular sassparilla drink.

Yellow Pond Lily
Nuphar variegata

ALSO CALLED Yellow Water Lily
FAMILY Water Lily (Nymphaeaceae)
ORIGIN Native
HEIGHT Aquatic
FLOWER Large, yellow, cup-like
LEAF Heart-shaped, floating
HABITAT Flooded swales. Perennial. Grows in the Ridges Sanctuary.

Nuphar comes from a Greek word that refers to a medicinal plant, and *variegata* means "variegated," possibly referring to the color of the sepals.

Yellow Pond Lilies require calm or slow-moving water since their roots are attached to the bottom of the pond bed. Channels in their stems and leaves trap air and keep the leaves and globe-shaped flowers afloat. Compared with the spreading petals of more familiar water lilies of the *Nymphaea* genus, the flowers of pond lilies never appear to be fully open.

The plant's large leaves provide resting places for frogs. Dragonflies, especially the Dot-tailed Whiteface, also rest on the leaves. Muskrats eat Yellow Pond Lily's rhizomes, and beavers and porcupines eat the entire plant.

Native Americans collected the rhizomes while they were green and pounded them into a mash, using it as a poultice to treat swollen limbs. They also dried the starchy rhizomes to make flour and roasted the seeds to eat as we eat popcorn today.

🍃 **CURIOSITY** *In England, men once believed that water lily rhizomes would cure the bite of a mad dog, and that if soaked in tar and applied to the head, they would cure baldness.*

Introduction to Lady's Slipper Orchids (*Cypripedium* Species)

The unusual beauty and slipper shape of the flower give Lady's Slippers their common name. The scientific name, *Cypripedium*, derives from two Latin words that loosely translate as "Venus slipper." Venus, a beautiful goddess, is sometimes called "Cypris" after the island of her birth. *Pedium* comes from the Latin word for "foot" and refers to the distinctive slipper shape of the flower.

Lady's Slippers grow in a variety of habitats, but the soil must be acidic and contain a specific type of underground fungus. The plants' seeds are the size of dust specks and are completely lacking in nutrients. The fungus in the soil attacks and digests the outer coating of the tiny seeds, allowing the inner cells to absorb nutrients from the fungus and eventually germinate—a process that takes several years. After germination, the plant and the fungus obtain nourishment from each other. Lady's Slipper seedlings may take up to 15 years to grow to flowering size. The sensitive and complex relationship between the orchid roots and the fungus makes transplantation nearly impossible.

Pollination of Lady's Slippers is a complicated procedure requiring insects, primarily bees, to enter the pouch-like flower. Once inside they often become trapped by its inward curving sides, some dying inside and some chewing their way out. Those that escape carry pollen to other Lady's Slippers. Research indicates that only a small percentage of the flowers are successfully pollinated each season. They owe their survival to their longevity. The average life span of a plant is 20 years, and some species may live for 100 years (provided they are not eaten by deer), giving them many opportunities to reproduce. Once a flower is pollinated, it is prolific, producing up to 60,000 seeds.

Early settlers and Native Americans used the powdered root of

Yellow, Pink and Showy Lady's Slippers to treat an assortment of ailments, including toothache, depression, insomnia, nervous disorders, epilepsy, alcoholic tremors, stomach ache, and the pain of childbirth. But beware! The hairy leaves and stems of some Lady's Slippers can cause painful blisters on the skin of those unwise enough to pick them.

Ram's Head Lady's Slipper
Cypripedium arietinum

FAMILY Orchid (Orchidaceae)
ORIGIN Native
HEIGHT 10"
FLOWER Small, whitish, veined with purple-red, pouch-shaped
LEAF Lance-shape, ribbed
HABITAT Shaded ridges, cold cedar swamps. Perennial. Grows in the Ridges Sanctuary.

THREATENED

When viewed from the front, Ram's Head Lady's Slipper looks a bit like the head of a charging ram, complete with horns. Its species name, *arietinum*, comes from the Latin word for "ram's head."

Ram's Head Lady's Slipper is the smallest and rarest *Cypripedium*. "Its beauty is greatly enhanced by the interlocking, two-toned purple veining on the sides of the pouch and the frothy, white cotton candy rim surrounding the opening at the top," said wild orchid hunter, Philip Keenan. This exquisite little orchid is difficult to find. Not only is it tiny (about the size of a fingertip) but it grows in dark places and usually occurs as a single flower, not a clump. Its short-lived blossoms appear wilted after being pollinated. Within an hour or two of pollination, the upper sepal droops, preventing other insects from entering the pouch.

Pink Moccasin Lady's Slipper
Cypripedium acaule

ALSO CALLED Moccasin Flower
FAMILY Orchid (Orchidaceae)
ORIGIN Native
HEIGHT 6–16"
FLOWER Large, pink, pouch-shaped
LEAF Basal, lance-shaped, ribbed
HABITAT Shrubby and shaded ridges. Perennial. Grows in the Ridges Sanctuary.

Native Americans gave this large pink flower its common name. The species name, *acaule*, means "stemless," referring to the way the leaves are attached to the stem.

Pink Moccasin Lady's Slipper usually produces only one flower per stem, but each flower lasts a long time. This elegant flower has become scarce in Wisconsin due to habitat destruction.

Yellow Lady's Slipper
Cypripedium calceolus, var. *pubescens*

FAMILY Orchid (Orchidaceae)
ORIGIN Native
HEIGHT 1–2'
FLOWER Large, yellow, pouch-shaped
LEAF Lance-shaped, ribbed, downy
HABITAT Ridges, rich woods. Perennial. Grows in the Ridges Sanctuary.

Calceolus is Latin for "small shoe," and *pubescens* means "becoming downy," referring to the stem and leaves.

Fragrant Yellow Lady's Slippers are the most abundant of the Lady's Slipper orchids.

Showy Lady's Slipper
Cypripedium reginae

FAMILY Orchid (Orchidaceae)
ORIGIN Native
HEIGHT 12–30"
FLOWER Large, white flushed with pink, pouch-shaped
LEAF Lance-shaped, ribbed, hairy
HABITAT Bogs, moist open areas near shore. Perennial. Grows in the Ridges Sanctuary.

SPECIAL CONCERN

Reginae means "queen," in Latin, so named because many consider *Cypripedium reginae* to be the most beautiful of all wildflowers.

Showy Lady's Slipper is the largest Lady's Slipper orchid. It requires more sunlight than other Lady's Slippers and can be found along trails, edges of woods, and even roadsides. Initially the plant produces only one flower. If not disturbed, it will produce more flowers in subsequent years, eventually forming a large clump. A clump with 20 flowers could be 100 years old—or even older.

In the early 1900s, bouquets of Showy Lady's Slippers were common altar decorations in rural churches, and children used the flowers as little boats, floating them in buckets of water. Today the plant is becoming increasingly rare. As far back as 1893, Mrs. William Starr Dana, noted wildflower author, predicted the Showy Lady's Slipper would eventually become extinct. Today scientists are not sure of all the reasons for its decline, but it is known that browsing deer and habitat loss are contributing factors.

❋ CURIOSITY *Showy Lady's Slipper is the symbol of the Ridges Sanctuary, and Yellow Lady's Slipper is the official flower of Door County.*

Canada Anemone
Anemone canadensis

ALSO CALLED Meadow Anemone
FAMILY Buttercup (Ranunculaceae)
ORIGIN Native
HEIGHT 1–2'
FLOWER White, 5 petal-like sepals
LEAF Hairy, deeply lobed, toothed
HABITAT Damp meadows, sandy shores. Perennial. Grows in the Ridges Sanctuary.

Anemone comes from a Greek word meaning "wind," probably referring to the way the leaves and stems of this genus bend and tremble in the wind. *Canadensis* means "of Canada."

Canada Anemone is taller than most anemones and blooms later. It spreads by sending out long underground roots, and as a result, often grows in large patches. Like other anemones, its seeds are dispersed by ants. (See page 14.)

Canada Anemone was prized by Native Americans who used it to treat many ailments. An infusion made from the roots was particularly valued in the treatment of eye problems, such as inflammation, crossed eyes, and cataracts. The Ojibwe used the herb to clear their throats before singing. Herbalists recommended the plant as a treatment for a diverse assortment of problems including headaches, gout, leprosy, eye inflammations, and ulcers. Today, modern herbalists discourage its use because of possible poisonous constituents.

🌿 CURIOSITY *An ancient legend says anemones appeared where Aphrodite's teardrops fell to the earth as she mourned the death of her beloved Adonis. She apparently wept copiously, since at least 25 species of anemone occur in North America.*

Twinflower
Linnaea borealis

FAMILY Honeysuckle (Caprifoliaceae)
ORIGIN Native
HEIGHT Ground-hugging vine with 3–6" flower stems
FLOWER Two, small, nodding, pink
LEAF Nearly round, notched, evergreen
HABITAT Shaded ridges and swales. Perennial. Grows in the Ridges Sanctuary.

Twinflower's blossoms always appear in pairs. *Linnaea* honors renowned botanist, Carolus Linnaeus, who discovered Twinflower in Lapland. He was so fond of the tiny plant that he had his portrait painted with it and suggested it be named for him, describing it as "a plant of Lapland, lowly, insignificant, disregarded, flowering but for a brief time—for Linnaeus who resembles it." *Borealis* means "of the north."

Twinflowers grow in cool woods and often form large colonies. Each dainty flower lasts approximately seven days, but the evergreen leaves may persist for two years. Twinflowers are easy to identify—the pairs of tiny pink flowers on thread-like stems are unmistakable.

FLOWER FACT Carolus Linnaeus, Father of Modern Botany

Carolus Linnaeus (1707–1778) developed the system of classifying and naming plants that is in use today. In his system, each plant has two names: the genus name (capitalized) followed by the species name (lowercase). The genus name covers an entire group of similar plants, while the species name is more specific, describing a particular plant's features, such as color, leaf size, where it grows, or honoring its discoverer. (See also page 71.)

Purple Avens
Geum rivale

ALSO CALLED Water Avens, Chocolate Root
FAMILY Rose (Rosaceae)
ORIGIN Native
HEIGHT 1–3'
FLOWER Drooping, 5 brownish-purple sepals
LEAF Toothed, divided into 3 lobes
HABITAT Shrubby ridges, edges of swales. Perennial. Grows in the Ridges Sanctuary and at Logan Creek.

"Avens" derives its name from the Latin *avencia*, a word of obscure origin. *Geum* means "to yield a taste of," probably because the roots of some species give off a clove-like scent. *Rivale* means "of riverbanks"—the plant's habitat.

Purple Avens, with its long stem and droopy flower, is rather weedy-looking. Its prominent purple sepals, and less visible yellow petals, enclose a bushy green center that later becomes a cluster of seeds. The seeds have tiny hooks at each end that readily attach to the fur of passing animals or the clothes of people—an efficient way for the plant to spread its seeds.

Early settlers called the plant "Chocolate Root" and used it to prepare a drink that looked like hot chocolate but tasted more like cloves. Mixed with sugar and milk, the concoction was used to treat dysentery and other gastric problems.

In medieval times, avens' three-lobed leaves were considered to symbolize the Holy Trinity and the five sepals to symbolize the five wounds of Christ. The plant was often portrayed in architectural decorations for church columns and walls.

🌿 CURIOSITY *The inventor of Velcro got his idea after walking in the woods and finding hooked seed pods (possibly from a species of avens) firmly attached to his clothes.*

Pitcher Plant
Sarracenia purpurea

ALSO CALLED Flytrap
FAMILY Pitcher Plant (Sarraceniaceae)
ORIGIN Native
HEIGHT 8–24"
FLOWER Large, nodding, purple-red
LEAF Basal, pitcher-shaped, reddish-green
HABITAT Open boggy swales. Perennial. Grows in the Ridges Sanctuary.

Pitcher Plant's hollow leaves resemble a hooded pitcher, giving rise to its common name. *Sarracenia* honors Michel Sarrasin de l'Etang, eighteenth century French physician and botanist, who discovered the plant in Quebec while serving as king's physician for the French Colony. *Purpurea* is Latin for "purple," referring to the color of the flower and leaves.

Pitcher Plants flourish in the Ridges' swales. Their umbrella-shaped flowers and pitcher-like leaves, usually partially filled with water and dead insects, make them easy to identify. The leaves of this carnivorous plant are designed to attract and trap insects. They are drawn to the leaves' colorful lips, crawl in, and drown in water that has collected there. If they are fortunate enough to escape drowning, they can't crawl out because the opening of the "pitcher" is lined with hairs that point downward. Although the plants secrete enzymes that help digest trapped insects, much of the breakdown is a result of bacterial activity. Pitcher Plants grow in bogs, which are typically low in available nitrogen, and thrive because they obtain sufficient nitrogen from the insects they "eat."

Pitcher Plant is not widely used as a medicinal plant, but it was once considered useful in treating stomach problems: "a teaspoonful of the plant to a cup of boiling water… drink cold, a large mouthful at a time."

Dwarf Enchanter's Nightshade
Circaea alpina

ALSO CALLED Alpine Enchanter's Nightshade
FAMILY Evening Primrose (Onagraceae)
ORIGIN Native
HEIGHT 3–10"
FLOWER Very small, white, 2 petals, in small cluster
LEAF Large, toothed, heart-shaped
HABITAT Swamps, damp woods. Perennial. Grows at Logan Creek.

Why this plant is called "Enchanter's Nightshade" is unclear because it is not a member of the Nightshade Family, and its little flowers would not ordinarily be called enchanting. The word "enchanting" derives from *Circaea*, named after Circe, an enchantress in Homer's *Odyssey*, who turned Ulysses' men into pigs and later became his lover. Circe is reputed to have used a poisonous species of this family to concoct magical potions. "Dwarf" refers to the plant's small size. It is almost a miniature version of Enchanter's Nightshade *(C. lutetiana)*. *Alpina* means "alpine."

Dwarf Enchanter's Nightshade thrives in cool temperatures. It is one of the few flowers that has just two petals. They are deeply notched and sit on a bulging green base that later becomes a burr. Hairs covering the base harden into hooked bristles that cling tenaciously to fur and fabric, thus dispersing its seeds. Jack Sanders, author and wildflower enthusiast, wrote that they… "annoy more woodland walkers with their pods than they enchant with their flowers."

Wild Rose
Rosa blanda

ALSO CALLED Smooth Rose
FAMILY Rose (Rosaceae)
ORIGIN Native
HEIGHT Shrub, 2–4'
FLOWER Pink, 5 petals, yellow stamens
FRUIT Large, red globe
LEAF Coarsely toothed, dull green
HABITAT Sunny, rocky, and sandy soil.
Perennial. Grows in the Ridges Sanctuary.

Rosa is Latin for "red," and *blanda* means "mild" or "thornless," distinguishing it from most other rose species. The common name, Smooth Rose, describes the plant's lack of thorns.

Wild Roses bloom in sunny spots in June, July, and August. The fruit, called "hips," forms in late summer and is a favorite food of birds. In autumn, the foliage turns orange and gold.

Roses, best known for their beauty and fragrance, are also a favorite of herbalists. Medicine made from the hips sooths body itch, and rose oil made from the petals has been used to treat every ailment from constipation to insomnia to sterility.

Rose petals are tasty and sweet and make a colorful garnish for salads. The hips, an excellent source of vitamin C, are sold in many natural food stores. Three rose hips are said to contain as much vitamin C as an orange.

Roses are considered a symbol of love and passion and have been cultivated as garden flowers for at least 2,000 years.

CURIOSITY *In the 1970s, a restaurant in Sturgeon Bay served rose hip soup.*

Red Osier Dogwood
Cornus stolonifera

FAMILY Dogwood (Cornaceae)
ORIGIN Native
HEIGHT Shrub, 3–10'
FLOWER White, flat-topped clusters on bright red twig
LEAF Pointed, pale underside, opposite
FRUIT Dull white
HABITAT Shrubby swales, moist meadows.
Perennial. Grows in the Ridges Sanctuary.

"Osier" means "red twigs." Some say the word, "dogwood," traces back to a brew made from its leaves that was used to wash fleas from dogs, and others say it comes from the old English word *dagge,* meaning "dagger." *Cornus* is Latin for "antler," referring to the hard wood of the tree, and *stolonifera* means, "a branch."

Red Osier Dogwood is a fast-growing shrub that spreads freely. It forms dense thickets that provide important cover for birds in the summer. At least eleven bird species eat the berries in late summer and fall. In winter, rabbits, chipmunks, and deer nibble on the twigs.

Early herbalists boiled dogwood bark to make an extract for washing itchy skin after exposure to poison ivy. The bark also served as a substitute for quinine during the Civil War. For centuries, Native Americans used young dogwood branches to make baskets, fish traps, cooking utensils, and frames for various implements. They also pulverized the red bark to make a dye.

FLOWER FACT Invasive Plants

Non-native plants, sometimes called invasives, exotics, or weeds, are considered a silent threat to our country's natural areas. They can move swiftly through plant communities, displacing native plants and degrading natural diversity. Non-native plants invading areas in Door County are purple loosestrife, garlic mustard, spotted knapweed, buckthorn, honeysuckle, helleborine orchid and phragmites.

| Apr | May | Jun | Jul | Aug | Sep | Oct |

Wild Columbine
Aquilegia canadensis

ALSO CALLED Canada Columbine
FAMILY Buttercup
  (Ranunculaceae)
ORIGIN Native
HEIGHT 1–3'
FLOWER Red with yellow centers, 5 spurs, nodding
LEAF Deeply lobed leaflets in groups of 3
HABITAT Open ridges, rocky places, edges of woods. Perennial. Grows in the Ridges Sanctuary and at Logan Creek.

"Columbine" comes from the Latin word for "dove." The five round petals, curving upward into closed spurs, are said to resemble a ring of five doves. *Aquilegia* may derive from the Latin for "to collect water," because water collects in the flower's hollow spurs. Or it may derive from the Latin for "eagle," because the spurs look slightly like the talons of an eagle. *Canadensis* means "of Canada."

Wild Columbine blossoms are perfectly designed for hummingbirds. Nectar is stored deep in the closed tips of the petals, discouraging insects and birds that do not have long tongues.

Wild Columbine contains prussic acid, which in small doses may have a narcotic or soothing effect on some people. The acid is toxic, however, although in the past the plant was used to treat one ailment or another. Tea made from powdered Wild Columbine seeds was used for headache, fever, and sore throat. Juice of the fresh plant was used to treat jaundice and abdominal pain. And the plant's leaves and flowers were supposed to cure measles and smallpox.

🌿 **CURIOSITY** *Wild Columbine was once suggested as our national wildflower, since its blossom resembles an eagle's talons.*

Blue Flag
Iris versicolor

ALSO CALLED Fleur-de-lis, Wild Iris
FAMILY Iris (Iridaceae)
ORIGIN Native
HEIGHT 3'
FLOWER Bluish-purple, 3 petals, 3 sepals with yellow crests
LEAF Basal, long, slender
HABITAT Wet swales, marshes, pond edges. Perennial. Grows in the Ridges Sanctuary and at Logan Creek.

The legend of Blue Flag's name dates back to the sixth century, when Clovis, king of the Franks, found his army backed up against the Rhine River by an army of Goths. According to the legend, he noticed a stand of iris growing in the river and realized the spot was shallow enough to cross. In gratitude for his escape, he adopted the iris as his family emblem. It ultimately became the emblem for all kings of France. After King Louis VII placed it on his flag during the Second Crusade (1147), it became known as the "Flower of Louis" or *Fleur de Louis*, shortened to fleur-de-lis.

Iris, the genus name, derives from Greek mythology. Iris was a messenger between the gods on Mt. Olympus and humans on earth. She used a rainbow to travel between the two worlds. When ancient Greeks saw a rainbow, they assumed Iris was delivering a message. *Versicolor* is Latin for "variously colored," referring to the multicolored flower.

It takes three years for a Blue Flag plant to progress from seed to flower. For the first two years the seedling yields only leaves, but by the third year the young plant usually produces a flower. Its leaves provide hiding places for waterfowl, and its blossoms provide nectar for hummingbirds, butterflies, and moths.

If consumed in quantity, Blue Flag's rhizome causes inflammation of the mucous membranes of the stomach and intestines. Nevertheless, Native Americans once considered it an important medicine and used it widely as a powerful cathartic, a means of eliminating internal parasites, a snakebite preventative, and a way to reduce obesity. Because of its toxic qualities, Blue Flag is not used as a medicine today.

Blue-Eyed Grass
Sisyrinchium montanum

FAMILY Iris (Iridaceae)
ORIGIN Native
HEIGHT 4–20"
FLOWER Small, violet-blue, yellow center, 6 pointed tepals
LEAF Grass-like
HABITAT Grassy meadows, roadsides. Perennial. Grows in the Ridges Sanctuary.

Blue-Eyed Grass is a misnomer — the plant actually has yellow "eyes" — but its flowers are very blue and its foliage is grasslike. *Sisyrinchium* means "swine snout," the Greek name for a similar plant whose roots were a favorite food of pigs. *Montanum* means "of the mountains." Although Blue-Eyed Grass does grow in the mountains, it grows in other places as well.

Don't expect to see this unconventional member of the Iris Family on a cloudy day, and even on a sunny day it can be difficult to find. The small flowers open only in sunshine, and the grass-like leaves and stems blend into their grassy habitat. The blossom's three petals and three sepals look alike and are called tepals.

The temptation to pick a lovely bouquet of Blue-Eyed Grass may be irresistible, but don't bother. The flowers close when picked.

Spikenard
Aralia racemosa

ALSO CALLED Spignet
FAMILY Ginseng (Araliaceae)
ORIGIN Native
HEIGHT 3–6'
FLOWER Very small, greenish-white, in clusters
FRUIT Conspicuous purple berries
LEAF Three branched parts of many heart-shaped leaflets
HABITAT Rich woods. Perennial. Grows at Logan Creek.

"Spikenard" is a translation of the Greek name, *nardostakhus*, but it is not related to the spikenard of antiquity (see below). *Aralia* was the name given to the plant by early French Canadians, and *racemosa* refers to the arrangement of a cluster of flowers or berries on a stem.

Spikenard, a very tall plant with very small flowers, is best known for its showy berries and its large, blackish roots. The roots have been used to treat an impressive variety of ailments. Nicholas Culpeper, English physician, apothecary, and astrologer (1616–1654), claimed "The roots boiled in wine or water, and drank, helps the stranguary and stoppings of the urine, the wind, swellings and pains in the stomach, pains of the mother, and all joint-aches. If the powder of the root be mixed with honey, and the same taken as a licking medicine, it breaks tough phlegm, and dries up the rheum that falls on the lungs."

❋ CURIOSITY *The spikenard mentioned in the Bible (precious ointment that Mary Magdalene poured over Jesus' feet) was believed to be the aromatic plant, Nardostachys jatamansi, of India.*

Lanced-Leaved Coreopsis
Coreopsis lanceolata

ALSO CALLED Longstalk Tickseed
FAMILY Daisy Family (Asteraceae)
ORIGIN Native
HEIGHT 1–2'
FLOWER Yellow, with darker yellow center
LEAF Lance-shaped
HABITAT Fields, roadsides, open ridges near beaches. Perennial. Grows in the Ridges Sanctuary.

Coreopsis derives from the Greek words *coris* meaning "a bug" and *opsis* meaning "appearance," describing the plant's seeds. *Lanceolata* means "lanceolate," referring to the shape of the leaves. The common name, Tickseed, describes the seeds that resemble black ticks.

Coreopsis is not fussy about where it grows. It tolerates thin, dry, or poor soil, often forming large colonies of bright, cheerful flowers that bloom throughout the summer. Its long bloom period and easy-to-grow qualities have made it an ideal garden plant.

Early settlers appreciated the plant for its effectiveness in repelling fleas and bedbugs in mattresses. The flowers make an outstanding dye, producing colors that range from yellow to rose-brown.

FLOWER FACT What Is a Wildflower?

"—nothing more than a blooming plant that can survive without our help. More than 10,000 kinds exist in North America, many of them rare and limited in territory, hundreds of them abundant and widespread. They range from odd-looking orchids whose locations are whispered only among trusted friends, to weeds that pop up in every lawn and garden… No matter what the design, wildflowers are always interesting and usually beautiful" (Jack Sanders, *Hedgemaids and Fairy Candles, The Lives and Lore of North American Flowers*).

Thimbleberry
Rubus parviflorus

ALSO CALLED Flowering Raspberry
FAMILY Rose (Rosaceae)
ORIGIN Native
HEIGHT 3–5'
FLOWER Large, white, 5 petals
FRUIT Raspberry-like
LEAF Very large, looks like a maple leaf
HABITAT Openings on shaded ridges. Perennial. Grows in the Ridges Sanctuary.

Similar in appearance to the thimble used for sewing, the cap-like fruit fits easily over the fingertip, thus the common name, Thimbleberry. *Rubus* means "to be red," referring to the color of the berry, and *parviflorus* means "small-flowered," a misnomer for a plant that produces such large blossoms.

Thimbleberry grows profusely in open woods all over Door County. At times, thickets of the plant are so dense that walking in wooded areas is nearly impossible. In the fall, Thimbleberry leaves turn brilliant orange to deep red.

The attractive red berries, surrounded by their big green leaves, look like delicious raspberries. Unfortunately, they squish easily when picked and are disappointingly tasteless, but with the addition of plenty of sugar, they make a decent jam.

🌿 CURIOSITY *Chewing Thimbleberry roots is said to remove tartar from teeth.*

Round-Leaved Sundew
Drosera rotundifolia

FAMILY Sundew
(Droseraceae)
ORIGIN Native
HEIGHT 4–8"
FLOWER Very small, white-pink, nodding, on threadlike red stem
LEAF Basal, round, covered with reddish hairs
HABITAT Hummocks in swales and bogs. Perennial. Grows in the Ridges Sanctuary.

In the sunlight, Sundew's leaves appear to be covered with glistening dew drops, hence its common name. *Drosera* means "dewy," and *rotundifolia* means "round-leaves."

Sundew is a tiny insectivorous plant. The glandular reddish hairs on its paddle-shaped leaves exude a sticky substance that traps and digests small insects. "The lightest touch of a living thing, a midge or a mosquito, causes the sundew leaf to react at once. Oddly, when the wind carries debris against the leaf, it does not respond" (Virginia S. Eifert, *Journeys in Green Places*). Sundew is better known for its deadly leaves (shown in the photo) than for its inconspicuous flowers. The entire plant is very small and blends into its boggy surroundings.

The sap of Sundew is so caustic that it was once used to remove warts and corns. Eighteenth century women mixed the sap with milk and used it to remove freckles. Early herbalists treated respiratory ailments with a tincture made of the sap mixed with water or wine—one teaspoonful of finely chopped Sundew in a pint of boiling water.

❦ CURIOSITY *The fluid secreted by Sundew's leaves is powerful enough to dissolve tooth enamel and cartilage.*

Tufted Loosestrife
Lysimachia thyrsiflora

ALSO CALLED Swamp Loosestrife
FAMILY Primrose (Primulaceae)
ORIGIN Native
HEIGHT Up to 30"
FLOWER Yellow, in fuzzy-appearing clusters along stem
LEAF Lanced-shaped
HABITAT Open ridges, open swales near beach. Perennial. Grows in the Ridges Sanctuary.

"Tufted" refers to the appearance of the flowers. The names "Loosestrife" and *Lysimachia* can be traced to the legend of Lysimachus, a king of ancient Sicily. The legend holds that the king waved a similar plant in front of a maddened bull that was chasing him, causing it to calm down or "loosestrife." *Thyrsiflora* is a Greek word describing the pyramidal arrangement of the individual flowers.

Tufted Loosestrife has a low tolerance for calcium and is usually found in peaty soil, such as that of the Ridges. The plant may be difficult to see because it is often shaded by taller vegetation. Tufted Loosestrife (Primrose Family) is not in the same family as the notoriously invasive Purple Loosestrife (Loosestrife Family).

Loosestrife of the Primrose Family has been put to an astonishing number of uses. During the American Revolution, it was politically incorrect to drink English tea, so dried loosestrife became the beverage of choice. Farmers found that tying a branch of the plant to the yoke of oxen helped repel gnats and other irritating insects. Pliny wrote that the odor of loosestrife would keep snakes away. Women made a juice from the flower to make blonde hair dye and used the crushed leaves to heal blisters caused by pinching shoes.

Indian Pipe
Monotropa uniflora

ALSO CALLED Corpse Plant
FAMILY Indian Pipe (Monotropaceae)
ORIGIN Native
HEIGHT 4–9"
FLOWER White, waxy, nodding
LEAF White scales on stem
HABITAT Shaded ridges. Perennial. Grows in the Ridges Sanctuary and at Logan Creek.

"Indian Pipe" describes the shape of the plant—its hanging flower resembles the bowl of a smoker's pipe. An old Indian legend says that the plant will appear on the forest floor wherever an Indian knocks the ashes out of his pipe. *Monotropa* means "one turn." When the plant begins producing seeds, the nodding flower slowly makes one turn upward. *Uniflora* means "one-flowered."

Indian Pipe is a saprophyte (see page 30), meaning it receives its nourishment from the decaying or rotting roots of other plants and doesn't require leaves or chlorophyll. The only vestiges of leaves are translucent white scales on the stem. When the plant has finished flowering, it turns black and eventually becomes dry and brown, often standing throughout the winter. Picking or touching the plant will also cause it to turn black. The common name, Corpse Plant, is well deserved because it is cool and clammy to the touch, and its bluish-white color is that of a corpse.

Native Americans used the plant, mashed and mixed with water, to heal sore and inflamed eyes. And as recently as the beginning of the twentieth century, it was used for that purpose by herbalists on the East Coast.

"It is the weirdest flower that grows," said Alice M. Earle, author of *Old-time Gardens*.

Highbush Cranberry
Viburnum opulus, subsp. *trilobum*

ALSO CALLED American Cranberry Bush
FAMILY Honeysuckle (Caprifoliaceae)
ORIGIN Native
HEIGHT Shrub, 3–9'
FLOWER White, in cluster
FRUIT Red
LEAF Toothed, 3 deep lobes
HABITAT Shady swales, cool moist woods. Perennial. Grows in the Ridges Sanctuary.

"Highbush Cranberry" received its common name because its berries closely resemble Thanksgiving cranberries. *Viburnum* is Latin for "wayfaring tree," and *opulus* means "a kind of maple," referring to the shape of its leaves.

The shrub's unusual flat-topped flower cluster is a ring of showy outer flowers surrounding much smaller interior flowers. The outer flowers have no stamens and are sterile. Only the interior flowers become fruit. Robins, cedar waxwings, ruffed grouse, brown thrashers, and cardinals feed on the fruit in the winter after they have exhausted other food sources. Bees use the blossoms for honey, and caterpillars of the Spring Azure Butterfly feed on the leaves.

The bright berries are rich in vitamin C but are mouth-puckeringly sour when eaten raw. When cooked with lemon peel (and plenty of sugar!), they make delicious jelly, sauce, or syrup.

Highbush Cranberry is an outstanding landscaping plant. In the fall, the leaves turn a rich burgundy color, and the bright red berries are beautiful against winter's snow.

Wood Nymph
Moneses uniflora

ALSO CALLED One-Flowered Shinleaf, Single Delight
FAMILY Shinleaf (Pyrolaceae)
ORIGIN Native
HEIGHT 2–6"
FLOWER White, nodding, on bent stem, fragrant
LEAF Basal, round, in rosette
HABITAT Shady ridges, damp woods with cool acidic soil. Perennial. Grows in the Ridges Sanctuary.

"Wood Nymph is aptly named. With a bit of imagination one can almost see a tiny boreal spirit hiding beneath each waxy, white flower," wrote naturalist Kathleen Harris, in the *Ridges News*. *Moneses* is a combination of Greek words meaning "single delight." *Uniflora* is Latin for "one flower."

The single flower, nodding at the tip of its curved stem, appears upside down when viewed from above. It's worth kneeling down to have a close look at the "face" of this unusual and charming blossom. It is perfectly organized into a pattern of fives—five petals, five sepals, five lobes at the tip of the pistil, and ten stamens. As the flower ages, it becomes more erect, lifting its face to the sky.

FLOWER FACT Warm Days in Mid-Winter

Why aren't plants fooled into sprouting by a warm spell in winter? Some are, but most rely on two cues to avoid false starts—hours of daylight and total hours of warm temperatures.

Green-Flowered Pyrola
Pyrola chlorantha

ALSO CALLED Greenish-Flowered Shinleaf
FAMILY Shinleaf (Pyrolaceae)
ORIGIN Native
HEIGHT Up to 10"
FLOWER Green, nodding
LEAF Basal, rounded ends, evergreen
HABITAT Moist, shaded ridges. Perennial. Grows in the Ridges Sanctuary.

Pyrola comes from a Greek word meaning "little pear," referring to the leaf shape of some species. *Chlorantha* is from a Greek word meaning "greenish."

This shade-loving plant, with its delicate, nodding flowers and evergreen leaves, is often found growing through pine needle mulch on the forest floor. Frequently last season's dried stems can be seen standing near the new blooming plants.

The leaves of plants in the Pyrola Family were once used to reduce the pain of bruises—often on the shins—resulting in the name, Shinleaf. The leaves were also used as a rheumatism treatment, a gargle for mouth sores, and as an eyewash. The remedies may have been effective because pyrolas contain a substance related to aspirin.

FLOWER FACT Evergreens

The leaves of many evergreen plants are... "glossy, leathery, and very durable. They are protected from excessive sun, cold, and wind by waxy layers of cells overlying the green, and by a supply of oils and sugars which add protection in cold... this sugar protects the plant's protoplasm from damage in low temperatures" (Virginia S. Eifert, *Journeys in Green Places*).

Pink-Flowered Pyrola
Pyrola asarifolia

ALSO CALLED Pink Shinleaf
FAMILY Shinleaf (Pyrolaceae)
ORIGIN Native
HEIGHT Up to 12"
FLOWER Pink, nodding
LEAF Basal, slightly heart-shaped, evergreen
HABITAT Moist, shaded ridges. Perennial. Grows in the Ridges Sanctuary.

Pyrola comes from a Greek word meaning "little pear," referring to the leaf shape of some species. *Asarifolia* refers to the supposed resemblance of the leaves of Pink-Flowered Pyrola to those of *Asarum* (Wild Ginger).

The fragrant, waxy blossoms of Pink-Flowered Pyrola, usually numbering between six and fifteen, grow along its leafless stem. Its basal leaves are dark green and shiny. The moist, sandy soil of the Ridges provides an ideal habitat for this delicate flower. There are many species of pyrola, and differences among some of them are minor.

FLOWER FACT Identifying Wildflowers

Pyrolas are one of many wildflowers that are challenging to identify. Habitat, soil fertility, and competition from nearby plants can cause subtle differences in plants of the same species. And some plants create complex taxonomic problems by hybridizing. Goldenrods, asters, and violets, for example, can display features of two similar species in one specimen.

Fireweed
Epilobium angustifolium

ALSO CALLED Great Willow Herb
FAMILY Evening Primrose (Onagraceae)
ORIGIN Native
HEIGHT 2–6'
FLOWER Deep pink, terminal spike
LEAF Narrow, pale underneath
HABITAT Opened woods, roadsides, clearings. Perennial. Grows in the Ridges Sanctuary.

Fireweed is one of the first plants to regenerate after a forest fire, hence its common name. *Epilobium* means "above the pod," referring to the manner in which the flowers bloom, starting at the bottom of the stalk and progressing upward, leaving behind small, cigar-shaped seed pods. *Angustifolium* means "narrow leaf."

Fireweed is a nectar source for many species of butterflies, particularly Red Admirals and Tiger Swallowtails. It also attracts bees in large numbers, and beekeepers have been known to move their hives to areas where Fireweed grows in abundance. Honey made from Fireweed nectar is delicately sweet and prized by connoisseurs.

Young shoots of the plant are a good substitute for asparagus and the young leaves, which are high in vitamin C, can be used in salads.

❋ CURIOSITY *Folklore says that when Fireweed blossoms reach the top of the stalk the first frost of the season will occur.*

Grass Pink
Calopogon tuberosus

ALSO CALLED Swamp Pink
FAMILY Orchid (Orchidaceae)
ORIGIN Native
HEIGHT 8–20"
FLOWER Magenta-pink, yellow-crested lip at top
LEAF Basal, single
HABITAT Open ridges, boggy swales. Perennial. Grows in the Ridges Sanctuary.

The plant's common name succinctly describes the grass-like single leaf and the vibrant pink blossoms. *Calopogon* means "beautiful beard," referring to the tuft of yellow-tipped hairs on the uppermost lip petal, and *tuberosus* refers to the plant's tuberous corm.

Grass Pink's flowers open sequentially, starting at the bottom of the stalk and moving upward. The fragrant flowers look upside down, with the bearded lip at the top, instead of at the bottom as with most orchids. Bees, thinking the yellow bristles on the lip are stamens, land on the hinged lip causing it to swing down, bringing them into contact with the plant's pollen.

"A wild rose torn to bits, then glued back together by someone who had never seen a flower before, might look something like a Grass Pink" (Raphael Carter).

FLOWER FACT Orchids

Orchids are often thought of as rare and fragile plants growing only in remote, lush, tropical rain forests. In reality, orchids grow on every continent except Antarctica—their habitats extend from the northern arctic tundra to the southernmost tip of South America. The Ridges Sanctuary harbors over 25 species of native, terrestrial orchids.

Self-Heal
Prunella vulgaris

ALSO CALLED Heal-All, Brunella
FAMILY Mint (Lamiaceae)
ORIGIN Introduced? Native?
HEIGHT 6–12"
FLOWER Small, violet, in spikes
LEAF Pointed, toothed, opposite
HABITAT Open areas. Perennial.

Grows in the Ridges Sanctuary and at Logan Creek.

The common name, Self-Heal, comes from the plant's purported cure-all ability. *Prunella* may derive from *brunella*, a German word referring to a mouth disease that infected German soldiers in the sixteenth century. Or *Prunella* may come from the Latin word for purple. *Vulgaris* means "common."

Self-Heal will grow nearly anywhere and is considered somewhat invasive. Early settlers may have brought it from Europe for medicinal purposes, but other authorities consider it native to both the United States and Europe.

Self-Heal was once a staple of herbal medicine. Each miniature blossom appears to have a throat and open mouth, and according to the Doctrine of Signatures (see page 12), it cured sore throats. In addition to its primary use as a treatment for sore throats, the fresh leaves were used as a poultice to stop bleeding and promote healing of wounds, burns, and hemorrhoids. And like many other herbs, it was supposed to be good for gastro-intestinal problems. Today, its healing powers have been discredited.

🌿 **CURIOSITY** *Mountain people in North Carolina refer to Self-Heal as "ground hog mustard" and use it to add flavor to mixed greens.*

Harebell
Campanula rotundifolia

ALSO CALLED Bluebells of Scotland, Witch's Bells
FAMILY Bellflower (Campanulaceae)
ORIGIN Native
HEIGHT 6–20"
FLOWER Nodding, blue-violet, threadlike stem
LEAF Long, narrow (round basal leaves disappear before flowering)
HABITAT Open ridges, rocky shores, meadows. Perennial. Grows in the Ridges Sanctuary and at Logan Creek.

Folklore held that witches used juice from Harebells to transform themselves into hares, thus its common name. *Campanula* means "small bell," and *rotundifolia* means "round-leaved."

Harebell's delicate flowers and threadlike stems belie its hardiness. Although it flourishes in the friendly environment of the Ridges Sanctuary, it also grows in less hospitable places. Its graceful blue flowers bloom all summer and into fall. Harebells have only minor medicinal value, but the flowers are said to make a good quality blue dye.

"I lingered round [the graves], under that benign sky: watched the moths fluttering among the heath and hare-bells; listened to the soft wind breathing through the grass; and wondered how anyone could ever imagine unquiet slumbers for the sleepers in that quiet earth" (Emily Brontë, final scene of *Wuthering Heights*).

CURIOSITY *Harebell is the plant badge for the MacDonald clan of Scotland.*

Wood Lily
Lilium philadelphicum

ALSO CALLED Orange Cup Lily
FAMILY Lily (Liliaceae)
ORIGIN Native
HEIGHT 1–3'
FLOWER Erect, orange-red, with purple-brown spots
LEAF Narrow, whorled around stem
HABITAT Open and shady ridges, roadsides, dry woods. Perennial. Grows in the Ridges Sanctuary.

The plant received its common name, Wood Lily, because it often grows in the forest openings of dry deciduous and coniferous woods. *Lilium* is Latin for "lily," and *philadelphicum* means "of Philadelphia."

Wood Lily's flower faces upward rather than nodding like most lilies. If it weren't for the gaps between the lower parts of its petals, rain would collect at the bottom of the flowers and damage the pollen.

Native Americans and early settlers chewed and pulverized the entire plant to make a paste they applied over spider bites. Romans supposedly cured corns with juice of the lily bulb. (Question: How did they develop corns if they wore sandals?)

"…consider the lilies of the field, how they grow; they toil not, neither do they spin; and yet I say unto you, that even Solomon in all his glory was not arrayed like one of these" (Matthew 6:28–29).

Black-Eyed Susan
Rudbeckia hirta

ALSO CALLED Brown Betty
FAMILY Daisy (Asteraceae)
ORIGIN Native
HEIGHT 1–3'
FLOWER Yellow, brown center, hairy stem
LEAF Rough, hairy
HABITAT Open ridges, fields, open woods. Annual/Biennial/Perennial. Grows in the Ridges Sanctuary.

Who was Susan and why was a flower named for her? Both are mysteries. But there is no mystery about *Rudbeckia*. It is the name given by Linnaeus in honor of Olaf Rudbeck, professor of botany at Upsala University in Sweden. At a time when Linnaeus was so poor he had to line his shoes with paper to cover the holes, Rudbeck gave him a job. *Hirta* means "hairy" and refers to the stem and leaves.

Black-Eyed Susan's bright yellow petals attract pollinating insects in summer, and its seeds provide winter food for birds, such as sparrows, cardinals, and chickadees.

Herbalists have used the plant to treat skin infections, and scientists have discovered it may have antibiotic properties. Excellent natural dyes, with colors ranging from beige to rich brown, can be made from Black-Eyed Susan blossoms.

FLOWER FACT

Carolus Linnaeus, Father of Modern Botany

As a young man, Linnaeus began writing careful descriptions of every plant he saw, notes that became the basis for his naming system (see page 47). In 1732 he undertook a five-month collecting trip in Lapland where he walked nearly 1,000 miles. His book, *Species Plantarun*, published in 1753, is considered the foundation of modern botanical nomenclature. For nearly a century he was a commanding figure in the scientific world, and even today his name is synonymous with plant knowledge and identification.

Common Mullein
Verbascum thapsus

ALSO CALLED Flannel Plant, Candle Wick, Jacob's Staff, Hag's Torch, Quaker Rouge, Camper's Toilet Paper (Common Mullein has accumulated more than 40 names.)
FAMILY Figwort (Scrophulariaceae)
ORIGIN Introduced
HEIGHT 2–6'
FLOWER Yellow, tightly packed cluster on spike-like stem
LEAF Velvety, basal rosette
HABITAT Fields, roadsides. Biennial. Grows in the Ridges Sanctuary and at Logan Creek.

The plant's common and scientific names all have hazy origins. "Mullein" comes from a Latin word, or it may be an old French word, meaning "soft." *Verbascum* may be an ancient Latin word for the plant, and *thapsus* may refer to an obscure Greek Island.

Common Mullein is a biennial. The first year, a large rosette of wooly leaves develops. Protected by velvety hairs, the leaves stay green all winter. The second year, a tall flowering stem arises. The thick, wooly stem produces tightly packed flower buds arranged somewhat like kernels on an ear of corn. The buds open a few at a time, becoming small yellow flowers. Long after the plant finishes flowering its stem remains upright, providing birds, especially Goldfinches, with seeds.

Over the years Common Mullein has been used as a medicine, an insulator, an illuminator, a cosmetic, and a walking implement. Most medicinal uses involved its leaves, particularly mullein tea, once widely used as a treatment for coughs, colds, and lung diseases. The velvety-soft leaves were used to sooth sunburn and applied to the head to alleviate headaches. In the 1800s, they were used like flannel to rub on rheumatism-inflamed joints. Colonists and Native Americans lined their footwear with leaves to keep out the cold.

The tall, stiff stems have nearly as many uses as the leaves. Roman soldiers dipped them in grease to use as torches, miners in the Old West used them for candles, and witches were said to use them to illuminate their sinister rites. The sturdy dried stems have been used as walking sticks since colonial times.

Mullein has fanciful uses too. Quaker women, whose religion forbade the use of cosmetics, rubbed the soft leaves on their cheeks to redden them, and Roman women used the flowers to make blonde hair dye. At one time the seeds were considered slightly narcotic and were thrown into water to make fish sluggish and easier to catch. Today, spring rosettes of Mullein leaves are often used in flower arrangements.

Death Camas
Zigadenus elegans

ALSO CALLED White Camas, Elegant Camas
FAMILY Lily (Liliaceae)
ORIGIN Native
HEIGHT 1–3'
FLOWER Greenish-white, star-shaped
LEAF Basal, grass-like
HABITAT Open and shrubby ridges, sandy beaches. Perennial. Grows in the Ridges Sanctuary.

The common name, Death Camas, refers to the poisonous properties of the plant. *Zigadenus* is composed of two Greek words meaning "paired glands," referring to the two glands at the base of each tepal (petal), and *elegans* is Latin for "elegant."

All North American species of the *Zigadenus* genus are poisonous to a greater or lesser degree. *Z. elegans* is less poisonous than some species, but nevertheless should not be eaten. The entire plant contains an alkaloid that in humans can cause low blood pressure, coma, dizziness, and slow heart rate. Sheep and cattle have been poisoned by grazing on the plant in early spring before other forage was available.

Yarrow
Achillea millefolium

ALSO CALLED Soldier's Woundwort, Milfoil
FAMILY Daisy (Asteraceae)
ORIGIN Introduced
HEIGHT 1–3'
FLOWER Very small, white, in flat-topped clusters
LEAF Gray-green, fernlike
HABITAT Open areas, fields, roadsides. Perennial. Grows in the Ridges Sanctuary and at Logan Creek.

The name, Yarrow, may come from an Anglo-Saxon word meaning "to prepare" or "to be ready," but another theory holds the plant was named after the River Yarrow in Scotland. *Achillea* is reputed to come from Achilles' use of Yarrow to heal his wounded soldiers during the Trojan War. *Millefolium* means "thousand leaves," referring to the many divisions of the plant's leaves.

Yarrow has been used medicinally throughout the world for centuries. Colonists brought it to America. They used the leaves, known for their strong herbaceous aroma, as a tea to treat colds, coughs, earache, fever, melancholy, loss of appetite, and diarrhea. Applied as a poultice, the tea was said to staunch the flow of blood. Washing the head regularly in the tea was also supposed to cure baldness, and chewing the leaves was thought to cure toothaches.

In Sweden, Yarrow was used in brewing beer, and Linnaeus (see page 47) claimed beer made with Yarrow was more intoxicating than beer made from hops. Yarrow is also rumored to be the main ingredient in witch's brew.

Chicory
Cichorium intybus

ALSO CALLED Coffee Weed, Wild Endive
FAMILY Daisy (Asteraceae)
ORIGIN Introduced
HEIGHT 1–4'
FLOWER Striking shade of blue
LEAF Basal leaves dandelion-like, upper leaves inconspicuous
HABITAT Grows almost anywhere in full sun. Perennial. Grows in the Ridges Sanctuary.

"Chicory" comes from *Cichorium*, the Arabian name for the plant, and *intybus* means "relating to chicory."

Chicory was brought to the United States in 1785 as a farm crop. Today it can be seen growing along roadsides, in fields, and even in the cracks of sidewalks. Its flowers open in the morning, usually fold by noon, and by the time darkness approaches, they have fallen off. The next morning new buds open at random places along the stem, each lasting only one day. Goldfinches and other songbirds love Chicory seeds and feed on the plants until every seed is gone.

Chicory is well-known as a food source. Its young leaves, high in vitamins and minerals, are excellent in salads and are a major export of Belgium. The big demand for Chicory, however, is its root, which is dried, roasted, ground, and made into a coffee-like beverage.

FLOWER FACT Introduced Plants

Many non-native plants, such as Chicory and Yarrow, were brought to America from Europe for specific purposes. Some of these introduced plants, however, have become invasive pests. A few plants have made the trip in the reverse direction. Black-eyed Susan, for instance, was exported to Europe as a garden flower.

✿ **CURIOSITY** *In New Orleans, chicory-blend coffee served with beignets is a popular treat at any time of day.*

Bulb-Bearing Water Hemlock
Cicuta bulbifera

ALSO CALLED Bulbous Water Hemlock
FAMILY Carrot (Apiaceae)
ORIGIN Native
HEIGHT 1–4'
FLOWER White, inconspicuous, in very small clusters
LEAF Narrow, bulblets in upper axils
HABITAT Swales, marshes, wet meadows. Perennial. Grows in the Ridges Sanctuary.

Cicuta is the Latin name for a poison hemlock plant, and *bulbifera*, loosely translated from Latin, means "bulb-bearing."

Bulb-Bearing Water Hemlock has little bulblets clustered in the axils (angles formed by the leaves and the stem) of its upper leaves. The entire plant is highly toxic, and some authorities consider it and its close relative, Water Hemlock *(Cicuta maculata)*, to be the most poisonous plants growing in this country. Symptoms of Water Hemlock poisoning begin shortly after ingestion. Excessive salivation is followed by tremors, violent convulsions, delirium, and death. Water Hemlocks are even more deadly than Poison Hemlock *(Conium maculatum)*, the plant used to poison Socrates.

Water Parsnip *(Sium suave)* is a similar appearing plant that also grows in the Ridges Sanctuary. The roots of Water Parsnip are edible, but because of their close resemblance to the poisonous roots of Bulb-Bearing Water Hemlock, a mistaken identification could be deadly.

🌿 **CURIOSITY** *Water Hemlock was the murder weapon used in **Missing Joseph**, a novel by Elizabeth George. The murderer claimed to have confused it with Water Parsnip.*

Common Evening Primrose
Oenothera biennis

FAMILY Evening Primrose (Onagraceae)
ORIGIN Native
HEIGHT 2–5'
FLOWER Yellow, 4 notched petals
LEAF Lance-shaped, wooly underside
HABITAT Beaches, fields, roadsides. Biennial. Grows in the Ridges Sanctuary.

"Evening" refers to the flower's habit of opening in late afternoon or evening, but "Primrose" is a misnomer—the plant is not a primrose. (The Evening Primrose Family is distinct from the Primrose Family.) *Oenothera*, loosely translated, means "wine-scented," a dubious reference to its fragrance, and *biennis* means "biennial."

Evening Primrose is one of the few plants whose flowers open at night. The plant is pollinated by moths and other night-flying insects, attracted to the blossoms' bright yellow color and heavy scent. By noon, the bedraggled and worn blossoms have wilted, and by evening, new buds begin opening for another night's activity. The plant's pods, similar in appearance to tiny bananas, contain seeds that are a favorite of many birds, particularly Goldfinches.

The seeds of Evening Primrose are rich in unsaturated fatty acids. There is some evidence that oil from the seeds may be useful in treating a number of medical conditions, including eczema, cirrhosis, rheumatoid arthritis, and elevated cholesterol levels.

All parts of Evening Primrose are edible, and in England this biennial is cultivated as a food plant. The beet-shaped roots are boiled, fried, or baked, much like parsnips. Young shoots can be used in salads, and the seeds can be crushed and baked into cakes.

Common Milkweed
Asclepias syriaca

FAMILY Milkweed (Asclepiadaceae)
ORIGIN Native
HEIGHT 2–6'
FLOWER Dusty pink, in slightly drooping clusters, fragrant
LEAF Oval, downy, gray underside
HABITAT Fields, roadsides.
Perennial. Grows in the Ridges Sanctuary and at Logan Creek.

"Milkweed" is named for the milky juice that oozes from its broken stems and leaves. *Asclepias* means "of Asclepios," the Greek god of medicine, and *syriaca* means "of Syria." Linnaeus (see page 47) mistook its country of origin when he named and classified this American plant in 1753.

Monarch Butterflies lay their eggs on milkweed. After the eggs hatch, the caterpillars spend their lives feeding on the plant's leaves. Upon reaching maturity, they build their jade-green chrysalises under the milkweed leaves. When the butterflies emerge, they feed on milkweed flowers. The sap ingested by the caterpillars is acrid, making them, as well as the emergent butterflies, distasteful to predatory birds.

Colonists discovered that the juice of Common Milkweed formed a tough adhesive covering for skin wounds—an instant bandage. Although some authorities now believe the roots are poisonous, both colonists and Native Americans used them to treat a variety of ailments. The sap is potentially dangerous too. It contains glycosides that can affect the heart, causing hot flashes, rapid heart rate, and general weakness.

Common Milkweed is well-known for its rough-textured pods,

tightly packed with overlapping seeds attached to long, silky down. When the pods split, the seeds open like parachutes and disperse into the wind. The silky down has been used in a surprising number of ways. Colonists used it to stuff pillows and mattresses, and in the 1860s thread made from the down was manufactured into netting, tapes, socks, and purses. During World War II, milkweed down was used extensively as a substitute for kapok in life preservers and the lining of airmen's flight suits. Milkweed down is five times as buoyant as cork, and a life jacket containing just a few pounds can hold up a 150-pound man in the sea. To help the war effort, Boy and Girl Scouts, civic groups, and farmers scoured the countryside for milkweed pods and shipped them to central collecting stations. In some places, milkweed farms were established, and harvesting the pods became a large-scale operation.

Swamp Milkweed
Asclepias incarnata

FAMILY Milkweed (Asclepiadaceae)
ORIGIN Native
HEIGHT 2–4'
FLOWER Deep pink, in clusters at top of stem
LEAF Lance-shaped
HABITAT Swamps, wet meadows. Perennial. Grows in the Ridges Sanctuary.

Incarnata is Latin for "flushed with pink."

The flowers of Swamp Milkweed are smaller and less fragrant than those of Common Milkweed, and their color is more intense. Like Common Milkweed, it is a host plant for Monarch Butterflies.

Native Americans found Swamp Milkweed to be a handy plant. Iroquois used fibers from the stems to make fish nets, and Pueblo Indians used them to weave fishing lines and sewing thread. Other Native Americans used a root tea to rid themselves of tapeworms.

Kalm's St. Johnswort
Hypericum kalmianum

ALSO CALLED Shrubby St. Johnswort
FAMILY Mangosteen (Clusiaceae)
ORIGIN Native
HEIGHT 2–3'
FLOWER Yellow, 5 petals, conspicuous stamens
LEAF Blue-green, edges rolled under
HABITAT Open ridges, shrubby swales near beaches. Perennial. Grows in the Ridges Sanctuary.

"Kalm" refers to Peter Kalm (see page 81), the plant's discoverer, and "St. John" refers to John the Baptist. Many years ago this plant was burned on St. John the Baptist's feast day (June 24) to protect farms and farm animals from evil spirits. "Wort" is a name given to plants used for medicine. *Hypericum* is Greek for "above a picture," alluding to the custom of hanging flowers over religious images or pictures on June 24. *Kalmianum* is another reference to Peter Kalm.

Kalm's St. Johnswort is a hardy plant of the Great Lakes region. Its blue-green foliage and brilliantly colored blossoms have made it a desirable landscape plant. This handsome native species is sometimes confused with the invasive introduced species, Common St. Johnswort *(Hypericum perforatum)*.

At one time, St. Johnswort was thought to cure those possessed by demons. Today, some species of St. Johnswort are used in antidepressant medications.

| Apr | May | Jun | Jul | Aug | Sep | Oct |

Kalm's Lobelia
Lobelia kalmii

ALSO CALLED Brook Lobelia
FAMILY Bellflower (Campanulaceae)
ORIGIN Native
HEIGHT 6–18"
FLOWER Small, bluish-purple with white throat
LEAF Very narrow
HABITAT Shrubby swales near beach, wet places. Perennial. Grows in the Ridges Sanctuary.

"Lobelia" is named after botanist, Matthias de L'Obel (known as Lobelius), physician to James I of England in the seventeenth century. "Kalm" and *kalmii* refer to Peter Kalm (see below).

Lobelia stems exude a bitter, milky juice called "lobelin" that is somewhat toxic. The wispy plants are lovely to look at but should never be eaten or used internally for medicinal purposes.

FLOWER FACT Peter Kalm

Peter Kalm, one of the great botanists of all time, was a student of Carolus Linnaeus. In 1748, the Swedish Academy of Science sent him to America to explore plant life and obtain seeds of useful plants that were hardy enough to withstand the climate of Sweden. For four years, he traveled extensively in eastern North America. The book he wrote about his experiences, *Travels into North America*, includes his observations about such things as household remedies, wearing apparel, public institutions, manners, food, customs of Native Americans, trade, and the political climate. He wrote, "I found everywhere the wisdom and goodness of the Creator; but too seldom saw any inclination among men to make use of them."

Spurred Gentian
Halenia deflexa

FAMILY Gentian (Gentianaceae)
ORIGIN Native
HEIGHT 8–24"
FLOWER Small, green, 4 spurs, in loose cluster
LEAF Paired, prominent lengthwise veins
HABITAT Shrubby ridges, trail edges. Annual. Grows in the Ridges Sanctuary.

"Spurred" in the plant's common name refers to the four projecting spurs on each flower, and "Gentian" refers to Gentius, King of Illyria (180–167 B.C.). According to Roman naturalist Pliny, King Gentius discovered the medicinal value of gentian roots when he used the plant to cure a mysterious illness that infected his troops. Linnaeus (see page 47) named the plant, *Halenia*, after his pupil, Jonas Halenius, who described the species in 1750. *Deflexa* means "bent downward" in reference to the flower's spurs.

FLOWER FACT Gaps in the Forest Canopy

Sunny gaps in the forest, whether man-made or the result of natural forces, provide spots that allow sun-loving plant species to germinate and grow. Windfall, disease, lightning strikes, and even trail construction can create these openings.

Spurred Gentian's green flowers, clustered at the top of its stem, are sometimes tinged with purple. The four downward-pointing spurs are hollow tubes formed at the base of the fused petals. This cool-climate plant thrives in the moist soil of the Ridges Sanctuary. In mid-to-late summer, its unusual flowers can readily be seen along partially sunny trail edges.

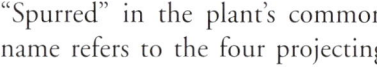

Joe Pye Weed
Eupatorium maculatum

ALSO CALLED Spotted Joe Pye Weed
FAMILY Daisy (Asteraceae)
ORIGIN Native
HEIGHT 2–5'
FLOWER Pink, flat-topped cluster, purple-spotted stem
LEAF Lance-shaped, toothed, whorled around stem
HABITAT Damp thickets, meadows. Perennial. Grows in the Ridges Sanctuary.

Joe Pye, a traveling Indian medicine man of the late 1700s, was reputed to have used this plant to cure typhus. Although the existence of Joe Pye is in doubt, the story lives on. *Eupatorium* refers to Mithridates Eupator, King of Parthia (120–63 B.C.). Eupator believed the plant was an antidote to poison and used it regularly as protection from the enemies—including his mother—who wanted to poison him. When his enemies eventually captured him, he preferred death to prison. He tried to poison himself, but he had previously consumed such a large quantity of his "antidote" that the attempt failed. In the end, he had to recruit a comrade to stab him to death. *Maculatum* means "marked with spots."

Joe Pye Weed is a tall, sturdy, handsome plant that blooms in late summer. It is frequently planted in butterfly gardens, where its clusters of tightly packed flowers are an important nectar source for many species of butterflies. Monarch Butterflies feed on the flowers prior to their long migration to Mexico.

Native Americans used fresh leaves from the plant as a burn poultice and made a root tea to bathe fretful children at bedtime. Nineteenth century Americans used the root to treat urinary infections and the leaves to treat a variety of ailments, including arthritis and impotence.

Pearly Everlasting
Anaphalis margaritacea

FAMILY Daisy (Asteraceae)
ORIGIN Native
HEIGHT 1–3'
FLOWER Pearly-white with yellow tuft at center, in clusters on wooly white stem
LEAF Narrow, gray-green on top, wooly white below
HABITAT Edges of trails, roadsides, meadows. Perennial. Grows in the Ridges Sanctuary.

"Pearly" describes both the shape and color of the blossoms, and "everlasting" is a fitting description of a plant that looks the same dried as fresh. *Anaphalis* is the Greek word for "everlasting," and *margaritacea* is the Latin word for "pearl."

Pearly Everlasting can survive in almost any well-drained soil and often forms widespread patches. The leaves have a pleasant lemon-lime fragrance, and the dried flowers retain their color, making them an excellent addition to dried floral arrangements. Thoreau called Pearly Everlasting "the artificial flower of the September pasture." It is a host plant for the American Painted Lady Butterfly.

Both Native Americans and colonists considered Pearly Everlasting to be a plant of exceptional utility. They used it to treat dysentery, heart problems, and paralysis, and as a poultice for sprains and bruises. Smoking dried leaves was a pleasant pastime as well as a treatment for asthma. Some medicine men believed anyone who chewed the leaves would want to sing, and the Cheyenne applied dried powdered leaves between their horses' ears and on the bottoms of the hooves to give them speed and endurance.

Touch-Me-Not
Impatiens capensis

ALSO CALLED Jewelweed
FAMILY Touch-Me-Not (Balsaminaceae)
ORIGIN Native
HEIGHT 2–5'
FLOWER Dangling, orange with reddish-brown spots
LEAF Oval, toothed
HABITAT Shores, wet woods. Annual. Grows in the Ridges Sanctuary and at Logan Creek.

"Touch-Me-Not" accurately describes the explosive reaction of the plant's seedpods when touched. *Impatiens* is from the Latin for "impatient," also referring to the seed pods, and *capensis* comes from the Cape of Good Hope, where the plant was mistakenly believed to have originated.

The cleverly designed seedpods of Touch-Me-Not shrink as they age. When disturbed, they pop open, scattering seeds in all directions. A high percentage of the plant is water. When it dies, it quickly dries up and a few weeks later all traces of it have disappeared. It is an important food source for Ruby-throated Hummingbirds and is a host plant for the American Painted Lady Butterfly.

Touch-Me-Not is well known as a balm to sooth poison ivy's itch. Here's the recipe. Cram as many leaves, stems, and flowers as possible into a pot with enough water to cover, and boil until the water turns bright orange. Put in a bottle and keep in the refrigerator. It relieves the itch and clears up the rash. Or, simply rub leaves on the affected areas. Strangely enough, Touch-Me-Not and Poison Ivy often grow in the same area.

The plant is frequently called "Jewelweed," perhaps because sun glinting off dew on the pale green leaves forms jewel-like droplets, or perhaps it's because the dangling flowers look like earrings.

Wild Bergamot
Monarda fistulosa

ALSO CALLED Horse Mint
FAMILY Mint (Lamiaceae)
ORIGIN Native
HEIGHT 2–4'
FLOWER Violet or pink, tubular, in large cluster
LEAF Pointed oval, toothed
HABITAT Dry meadows. Perennial. Grows in the Ridges Sanctuary.

When crushed, Wild Bergamot leaves have a citrus-mint scent that resembles the smell of bergamot oranges, grown around Bergamo, Italy. Oil from the oranges is used to make perfume and flavor foods, such as Earl Gray Tea. *Monarda* refers to Nicholas Monardes, a sixteenth century Spanish physician who wrote a comprehensive book on the medicinal values of New World plants. *Fistulosa* means "full of pipes," describing the long florets.

Wild Bergamot's fragrant flowers attract numerous varieties of bees and butterflies. Hummingbirds, too, are drawn to the tubular flowers. The flowers vary in color from violet to pink, depending on soil and growing conditions.

Native Americans used boiled bergamot leaves to treat acne and fresh leaves to treat insect bites. They drank bergamot tea to relieve headaches, colds, and sore throats.

Colonists used tea made from dried bergamot leaves as a substitute for imported tea. They room-dried the leaves for several weeks, then stored them in glass jars in a dark place. When they were thirsty, they steeped ¾ teaspoon of crushed leaves in one cup of boiling water—and enjoyed the refreshing taste of Wild Bergamot tea.

Wild Bergamot is often mistakenly called Oswego Tea or Bee Balm, but these are names for a related plant, *Monarda didyma*, that has red (not pink) flowers.

Nodding Ladies Tresses
Spiranthes cernua

ALSO CALLED Pearl Twist
FAMILY Orchid (Orchidaceae)
ORIGIN Native
HEIGHT Up to 24"
FLOWER White, slightly nodding, in spike
LEAF Basal, grasslike
HABITAT Open ridges near beach. Perennial. Grows in the Ridges Sanctuary.

"Ladies Tresses" describes the arrangement of this orchid's spiraling flowers. They appear woven into the stem and resemble a lady's braid or "tress." *Spiranthes* is a combination of two Greek words meaning "spiral flower," and *cernua* is the Latin word for "nodding" or "turned towards the earth."

Bees are drawn to the exceedingly fragrant flowers of Nodding Ladies Tresses. When a bee visits, it starts at the bottom of the spiral spike and works its way to the top. It then moves on to the next spike and repeats the performance. Slender Ladies Tresses and Hooded Ladies Tresses also grow in the Ridges Sanctuary. Distinguishing among the three species of *Spiranthes* can be difficult.

🍀 **CURIOSITY** *Orchids were named for Orchis of Greek mythology, son of a nymph and satyr. He was not an attractive fellow! Unfortunately, he was overly ardent. After imbibing too freely at a festival of Bacchus, he assaulted a priestess. In turn, angry revelers attacked him, tearing him limb from limb. His father prayed the gods would put him back together, but they refused, saying he was so obnoxious during life, they wanted him to bring pleasure after death—so they turned him into an orchid!*

Wintergreen
Gaultheria procumbens

ALSO CALLED Teaberry, Chickaberry
FAMILY Heath (Ericaceae)
ORIGIN Native
HEIGHT 2–8", creeper
FLOWER White, bell-shaped, nodding
FRUIT Bright red
LEAF Oval, leathery, becoming red-bronze in winter
HABITAT Shrubby ridges, moist woods. Perennial. Grows in the Ridges Sanctuary.

"Wintergreen" succinctly describes this evergreen plant. Linnaeus (see page 47) named it *Gaultheria* in honor of Dr. Jean-François Gaulthier, an eighteenth century Canadian botanist and physician. *Procumbens* means "reclining."

Wintergreen grows so plentifully in the Ridges Sanctuary that it has a trail named after it. In summer, bees collect pollen from its flowers, and in winter, birds eat the long-lasting berries. Humans also like the berries and enjoy their breath-freshening taste. Chipmunks eat the berries, too. No doubt they have very sweet breath!

Most medicinal uses of wintergreen involve the minty-tasting leaves. Wintergreen tea is a refreshing drink, as well as a treatment for a variety of ailments. Methyl salicylate, an oil closely related to the principal chemical in aspirin, has been extracted from the wintergreen plant, and many of today's remedies for muscular pains contain oil of wintergreen.

CURIOSITY *Appalachian Mountain children took wintergreen leaves to church to chew during long sermons.*

Grass of Parnassus
Parnassia glauca

ALSO CALLED Bog Star
FAMILY Saxifrage (Saxifragaceae)
ORIGIN Native
HEIGHT 6–20"
FLOWER White with delicate blue-green veins, 5 petals
LEAF Basal, heart-shaped
HABITAT Open ridges and swales. Perennial. Grows in the Ridges Sanctuary.

The origin of the name, Grass of Parnassus, is unclear. The plant doesn't resemble grass, although the flowers do grow on long slender stems. "Parnassus" and *Parnassia* refer to Mt. Parnassus in Greece, where first century Greek physician, Dioscorides, apparently observed similar plants. Dioscorides, one of the earliest experts in the study of herbal medicine, was the author of *De Materia Medica*. The book covered 600 plant species and was the leading work on pharmacology for sixteen centuries. *Glauca* means "silvery" or "gleaming," referring to the flowers.

Grass of Parnassus favors wet, limey soils. This abundant, late-blooming plant often appears in the same spots where Dwarf Lake Iris and Arctic Primrose grew in the spring, and in late summer it can be seen dancing in the wind alongside its exquisite companion, Fringed Gentian.

Grass of Parnassus is not known for its medicinal uses, but Dioscorides claimed that a concoction of juice from the root mixed with wine, honey, myrrh, frankincense, and pepper made an excellent medicine for treating eye problems.

Ohio Goldenrod
Solidago ohioensis

FAMILY Daisy (Asteraceae)
ORIGIN Native
HEIGHT 2–3'
FLOWER Small, yellow, in flattish cluster
LEAF Narrow, lance-shaped
HABITAT Open ridges, swales near beach.
  Perennial. Grows in the Ridges Sanctuary.

SPECIAL CONCERN

Solidago: For meaning of this term see opposite page. *Ohioensis* means "of Ohio." Ohio Goldenrod, earliest blooming of the Door County goldenrods, can be identified by its flat-topped flower clusters.

| Apr | May | Jun | Jul | Aug | Sep | Oct |

Dune Goldenrod
Solidago simplex,
var. *gillmanii*

FAMILY Daisy (Asteraceae)
ORIGIN Native
HEIGHT Up to 4'
FLOWER Small, yellow, in spike, red stem
LEAF Narrow, wavy edge
HABITAT Sandy ridges, beaches. Perennial.
  Grows in the Ridges Sanctuary.

Simplex means "simple," and *gillmanii* refers to the plant's discoverer, Henry Gillman.

THREATENED

Dune Goldenrod's red stem makes it easy to identify. Nationally, it grows in only four states—Wisconsin, Michigan, Illinois, and Indiana. In Wisconsin, it occurs in only Door, Sheboygan, and Kewaunee counties.

Canada Goldenrod
Solidago canadensis

FAMILY Daisy (Asteraceae)
ORIGIN Native
HEIGHT 1–5'
FLOWER Small, yellow, in curved plumes
LEAF Lance-shaped, toothed
HABITAT Sunny fields, roadsides. Perennial. Grows in the Ridges Sanctuary and at Logan Creek.

Canadensis means "of Canada."

Canada Goldenrod is the most common Door County goldenrod. It is distinguished by the round galls that often form on its stem.

Goldenrod's common name describes the plant— the flowers are golden and the stems are rodlike. *Solidago* comes from a Latin word meaning "solidify," referring to the healing powers ancient physicians believed the plant possessed.

Up to 100 species of goldenrod grow in the United States. They are so widespread and bloom so profusely that in late summer they provide the dominant color in many fields and meadows. In winter, goldenrod is a source of seeds for a variety of birds.

The sunny yellow plant has given rise to many superstitions. The Meswaki Indians, for example, believed that some children are born without the ability to laugh. Washing them in goldenrod, boiled with the bone of an animal that died at the time the child was born, guaranteed the child the gift of laughter. Other superstitions equate goldenrod with gold, and thus wealth and good fortune.

The common perception that goldenrod causes allergic reactions isn't true. Goldenrod pollen is rather sticky and doesn't easily become airborne. Ragweed is the usual culprit.

🌿 CURIOSITY *Goldenrod contains small quantities of rubber, and at one time Thomas Edison conducted experiments to determine whether it would be economically feasible to use the plant commercially.*

Purple Gerardia
Agalinis purpurea

ALSO CALLED Smooth Agalinis
FAMILY Figwort (Scrophulariaceae)
ORIGIN Native
HEIGHT Up to 3'
FLOWER Pink to magenta, bell-shaped, growing in axils
LEAF Very narrow, opposite
HABITAT Moist meadows and beaches. Annual. Grows in the Ridges Sanctuary.

"Gerardia" honors renowned Elizabethan herbalist, John Gerard (1545–1612), author of *Great Herball or General Historie of Plants* (1597). This famous and entertaining book includes such hints as rubbing onion juice on a bald head in the sunshine to speedily restore hair, and giving a mixture of daisy juice and milk to puppies to keep them from growing too large. *Agalinis* is derived from a Latin word meaning "flax," and *purpurea* means "purple."

Each of Purple Gerardia's showy, bell-shaped flowers lasts only a day, sometimes fading by noon. Unfortunately, the beautiful flowers are a favorite browse for deer.

Medieval herbalist-physicians believed roots of Purple Gerardia (as well as other members of the Figwort Family) cured hemorrhoids. More recently, the roots have been used to make a tea to treat disorders of the stomach and bowels.

FLOWER FACT Annual/Biennial/Perennial

- Annual: a plant that completes its life cycle in one growing season.
- Biennial: a plant that lives for two years; the first year it stores food so that in the second year it can flower and produce seeds.
- Perennial: a plant that normally lives for more than two seasons and produces flowers each year.

Turtlehead
Chelone glabra

ALSO CALLED Snakehead, Balmony
FAMILY Figwort (Scrophulariaceae)
ORIGIN Native
HEIGHT 1–3'
FLOWER Large, white, in tight terminal cluster
LEAF Lance-shaped, toothed, opposite
HABITAT Swale margins. Perennial. Grows in the Ridges Sanctuary.

Viewed from the side, the plant's blossoms look like the head of a turtle, thus its common name. *Chelone* is Greek for "tortoise," and *glabra* is Latin for "smooth," describing the stem and leaves.

Blooming in late summer, the two-lipped flowers of this tall plant are unmistakable. The upper lip arches over the hairy lower lip, giv-

ing the appearance of a turtle with its mouth open. It takes a big, sturdy bumblebee to enter and pollinate a Turtlehead. When a bee, looking for nectar, squeezes between the closed lips and wiggles around inside, the lips open and close as if the flower were chewing.

Early settlers called the plant "Balmony" and made a balm (ointment) from the leaves to relieve itching and other skin irritations. The leaves were well-known to Native Americans who brewed them into a bitter tasting tea to use as a tonic and laxative.

Large-Leaf Aster
Aster macrophyllus

ALSO CALLED Big-Leaved Aster
FAMILY Daisy (Asteraceae)
ORIGIN Native
HEIGHT 1–4'
FLOWER White-to-blue, on purplish stem
LEAF Very large (up to 8"), heart-shaped.
HABITAT Dry deciduous and coniferous woods. Perennial. Grows in the Ridges Sanctuary.

Aster comes from a Greek word meaning "starry." *Macrophyllus* means "large leaved." The young leaves of this common aster are sometimes cooked and eaten like spinach.

Calico Aster
Aster lateriflorus

ALSO CALLED Side-Flowering Aster, Goblet Aster
FAMILY Daisy (Asteraceae)
ORIGIN Native
HEIGHT 1–4'
FLOWER White or purple-tinged, often one side of stem
LEAF Lance-shaped, slightly toothed
HABITAT Shaded and shrubby ridges. Perennial. Grows in the Ridges Sanctuary.

Calico Aster received its name because the blooming plant sometimes appears multi-colored. The ray flowers surround a yellow disk that turns purplish-red as the flower ages, making it possible to have both yellow and purple disks on a single plant. *Lateriflorus* means "one-side-flowering," referring to the fact that the flowers tend to grow on one side of the stem.

New England Aster
Aster novae-angliae

ALSO CALLED Michaelmas Daisy
FAMILY Daisy (Asteraceae)
ORIGIN Native
HEIGHT Up to 6'
FLOWER Purplish-blue, large yellow disk, hairy stem
LEAF Clasping
HABITAT Open fields, roadsides, woodlands. Perennial. Grows in the Ridges Sanctuary.

Novae-angliae means "New England. Although called "New England," this showy aster is widespread east of the Mississippi River. It is one of the tallest of the asters and the latest blooming. The late bloom period makes its flowers an important food source for migrating Monarch Butterflies.

Identification of asters is difficult even for an expert. Differences among species are often small, and the various species tend to hybridize. The three species shown in this book are relatively easy to identify.

Growing in clusters and sometimes thickly blanketing fields or roadsides, asters begin blooming in August. They continue to provide splashes of color until the short, cool days of October. The flowers' colorful petals are actually sterile florets known as "ray flowers." Their function is to attract insects. The center disk (usually yellow) contains fertile florets—tightly packed tiny flowers, known as "disk flowers."

Asters are not noted for their medicinal or practical value. Early colonists seldom used them, but Native Americans sometimes used asters to treat skin rashes, earaches, and stomach pains. They believed the smoke from smudged blossoms, when forced into the nostrils, would revive an unconscious person.

CURIOSITY *Where did asters come from? Legend has it they sprang up where the goddess Virgo scattered stardust on the earth.*

Beechdrops
Epifagus virginiana

ALSO CALLED Cancer Drops
FAMILY Broomrape
  (Orobanchaceae)
ORIGIN Native
HEIGHT 6–18"
FLOWER Small, tubular,
  maroon and white
LEAF Yellowish-brown scales
HABITAT Under beech trees.
  Annual. Grows at Logan
  Creek.

Beechdrop plants grow only under beech trees, thus the common name. *Epi* is from the Greek, meaning "upon," and *phagos* means "the beech." *Virginiana* means "of Virginia."

Beechdrops is a parasitic plant (see page 30) that receives its nourishment from the roots of beech trees and thus has no need for photosynthesis or green leaves. Its leaves are represented by yellowish-brown scales scattered along the stem. The wispy plant, with its unique flowers, is at first difficult to see, but once spotted, the well-camouflaged plants can be seen growing in abundance at Logan Creek. The dried plants persist into late fall and sometimes into the next summer.

Beechdrops is an astringent and has been used to treat skin conditions such as ulcers, bruises, cuts, and wounds. Mrs. Grieve, author of the widely quoted, *A Modern Herbal* (1931), claimed its use would arrest gangrene. Colonists made a bitter-tasting tea from Beechdrops that they used to treat dysentery, gonorrhea, and even cancer.

🍀 CURIOSITY *Molecular geneticists have discovered that Beechdrop plants contain remnants of the genetic material found in photosynthetic plants. This suggests that their ancestors were photosynthetic, but during their evolution they became totally dependent on their host plant (beech) for nutrition. Perhaps they evolved in dark places where sunlight was minimal.*

Lesser Fringed Gentian
Gentianopsis procera

FAMILY Gentian (Gentianaceae)
ORIGIN Native
HEIGHT 6–18"
FLOWER Blue, vase-shaped, fringed petals
LEAF Narrow, partly folded.
HABITAT Open ridges near beach. Biennial. Grows in the Ridges Sanctuary.

SPECIAL CONCERN

The plant's common and genus names are both derived from King Gentius (see page 82). *Procera* is Latin for "long" or "stretched out," referring to the flower's shape.

On cloudy days and at night, Fringed Gentian's flower petals curl tightly around the flower tube, protecting the interior. The fringed petals serve as a barrier to prevent crawling, non-pollinating insects from stealing the nectar. Because the fringe isn't strong enough to provide support, the insects fall off. Fringed Gentians are fussy about their habitat. They require soil that is moderately acidic and moist, but not wet.

Native Americans used a root tea made from gentians to purify the blood and strengthen the stomach, and herbalists used the tea for a wide variety of ailments including colds, skin rash, kidney stones, and bruises.

Poets and writers delight in describing Fringed Gentian's glorious color. William Cullen Bryant called it "heaven's own blue," and Thoreau described the color as, "surpassing that of the male bluebird's back."

Acknowledgments

For the excellent photographs:
Paul Burton, Bill May, Paul Regnier, and Janice Stiefel

For editing assistance:
Paul Burton, Bill May, Paul Regnier, and Fred Schwartz

For encouragement and support:
The Board of Directors and staff of the Ridges Sanctuary

For invaluable help in all phases of writing and photography:
Paul Burton

Sources of Quotes

Page xii, Walter Hagen quote, from *Bartlett's Familiar Quotations,* 1992 edition
Page 18, Susan Fenimore Cooper quote, from Coffey, *Wildflowers of North America*
Page 19, Susan Fenimore Cooper quote, from Coffey, *Wildflowers of North America*
Page 20, Physician quote and Maximillian quote, from Coffey, *Wildflowers of North America*
Page 22, Izaak Walton quote, from *The Compleat Angler*
Page 31, Definition of umbels, from *The Audubon Society Field Guide to North American Wildflowers*
Page 38, Thoreau quote, from Coffey, *Wildflowers of North America*
Page 47, Linnaeus quote, from Korling, *The Boreal Forest and Borders*
Page 49, Recipe for treating stomach problems, from Meyer, *The Herbalist*
Page 61, Alice M. Earle quote, from Sanders, *Hedgemaids and Fairy Candles*
Page 63, Kathleen Harris quote, from *Ridges News*, Summer, 1994, Vol. 20, Number 1
Page 84, Thoreau quote, from Edsall, *Roadside Plants and Flowers*
Page 97, Bryant and Thoreau quotes, from Sanders, *Hedgemaids and Fairy Candles*

Photo Credits

Page vi: Bob Ragotzkie
Page 1: Trailing Arbutus, Paul Burton
Page 2: Sharp-Lobed Hepatica, Paul Burton
Page 2: Round-Lobed Hepatica, Paul Regnier
Page 3: Bloodroot, Paul Burton
Page 4: Marsh Marigold, Paul Burton
Page 5: Lyre-Leaved Rock Cress, Janice Stiefel
Page 6: Canada Buffaloberry, Janice Stiefel
Page 7: Trout Lily, Paul Burton
Page 8: Long-Spurred Violet, Paul Regnier
Page 9: Pussytoes, Janice Stiefel
Page 10: Spring Beauty, Janice Stiefel
Page 11: Broad-Leaved Toothwort and root, Paul Burton
Page 11: Cut-Leaved Toothwort, Janice Steifel
Page 12: Bellwort, Paul Regnier
Page 13: Dutchman's Breeches, Paul Burton
Page 14: Wood Anemone, Paul Regnier
Page 15: Big White Trillium, Frances Burton
Page 16: Arctic Primrose, Paul Burton
Page 17: Dwarf Lake Iris, Paul Regnier
Page 18: Starflower, Paul Regnier
Page 19: Gaywings, Paul Burton
Page 20: Bearberry, Bill May
Page 21: Goldthread, Janice Stiefel
Page 22: Wild Strawberry, Paul Regnier
Page 23: Jack-in-the-Pulpit, Paul Burton
Page 24: Blue Cohosh, Janice Stiefel
Page 25: Indian Paintbrush, Janice Stiefel
Page 26: Canada Mayflower, Janice Stiefel
Page 27: White Baneberry, Janice Stiefel
Page 28: Starry Solomon's Plume, Paul Regnier
Page 29: Bog Rosemary, Janice Stiefel
Page 30: Cancer Root, Paul Regnier
Page 31: Bastard Toadflax, Bill May
Page 32: Buckbean, Paul Regnier
Page 33: Silverweed, Paul Regnier
Page 34: Sweet Cicely, Paul Burton
Page 35: Bunchberry, Janice Stiefel
Page 36: Clintonia, Janice Stiefel
Page 37: Swamp Buttercup, Janice Stiefel
Page 38: Labrador Tea, Paul Regnier
Page 39: Striped Coral Root, Paul Burton
Page 40: Wild Sarsaparilla, Janice Stiefel
Page 40: Wild Sarsaparilla close-up, Bill May
Page 41: Yellow Pond Lily, Paul Burton
Page 43: Ram's Head Lady's Slipper, Paul Burton
Page 44: Pink Moccasin Lady's Slipper, Paul Burton
Page 44: Yellow Lady's Slipper, Paul Burton
Page 45: Showy Lady's Slipper, Paul Regnier
Page 46: Canada Anemone, Paul Regnier
Page 47: Twinflower, Bill May

Page 48: Purple Avens, Paul Regnier
Page 49: Pitcher Plant, Paul Regnier
Page 50: Dwarf Enchanter's Nightshade, Bill May
Page 51: Wild Rose, Paul Regnier
Page 52: Red Osier Dogwood, Paul Regnier
Page 53: Wild Columbine, Janice Stiefel
Page 54: Blue Flag, Janice Stiefel
Page 55: Blue-Eyed Grass, Bill May
Page 56: Spikenard berries, Janice Stiefel
Page 57: Lance-Leaved Coreopsis, Janice Stiefel
Page 57: Lance-Leaved Coreopsis close-up, Paul Burton
Page 58: Thimbleberry, Janice Stiefel
Page 59: Round-Leaved Sundew, Paul Burton
Page 60: Tufted Loosestrife, Paul Regnier
Page 61: Indian Pipe, Janice Stiefel
Page 62: Highbush Cranberry, Janice Stiefel
Page 63: Wood Nymph, Bill May
Page 64: Green-Flowered Pyrola, Bill May
Page 65: Pink-Flowered Pyrola, Bill May
Page 66: Fireweed, Bill May
Page 67: Grass Pink, Paul Regnier
Page 67: Grass Pink close-up, Paul Burton
Page 68: Self-Heal, Bill May
Page 69: Harebell, Paul Burton
Page 70: Wood Lily, Bill May
Page 71: Black-Eyed Susan, Paul Burton
Page 72: Common Mullein, Paul Regnier
Page 73: Death Camas, Paul Regnier
Page 74: Yarrow, Paul Burton
Page 75: Chicory, Bill May
Page 76: Bulb-Bearing Water Hemlock, Janice Stiefel
Page 77: Common Evening Primrose, Janice Stiefel
Page 78: Common Milkweed, Janice Stiefel
Page 79: Swamp Milkweed, Paul Regnier
Page 80: Kalm's St. Johnswort, Paul Burton
Page 81: Kalm's Lobelia, Janice Stiefel
Page 82: Spurred Gentian, Paul Burton
Page 83: Joe Pye Weed, Paul Regnier
Page 84: Pearly Everlasting, Janice Stiefel
Page 85: Touch-Me-Not, Bill May
Page 86: Wild Bergamot, Bill May
Page 87: Nodding Ladies Tresses, Paul Burton
Page 88: Wintergreen, Janice Stiefel
Page 89: Grass of Parnassus, Paul Regnier
Page 90: Ohio Goldenrod, Paul Regnier
Page 90: Dune Goldenrod, Paul Burton
Page 91: Canada Goldenrod, Bill May
Page 92: Purple Gerardia, Bill May
Page 93: Turtlehead, Janice Stiefel
Page 93: Turtlehead and bee, Paul Burton
Page 94: Large-Leaf Aster, Janice Stiefel
Page 94: Calico Aster, Janice Stiefel
Page 95. New England Aster, Janice Stiefel
Page 96: Beechdrops, Paul Burton
Page 97: Lesser Fringed Gentian, Paul Burton

Bibliography

Adkins, Leonard M., 1999. *Wildflowers of the Appalachian Trail*, Menasha Ridge Press, Birmingham, Alabama.

Andrews, Jonathan, 1986. *Creating A Wildflower Garden*, published in England and reprinted by MJF Books, New York.

Case, Frederick, 1964. *Orchids of the Western Great Lakes Region*, Cranbrook Institute of Science, Bloomfield Hills, Michigan.

Clausen, Ruth R., 1999. *Fandex Guide to Wildflowers*, Workman Publishing Co., New York.

Coffey, Timothy, 1993. *History and Folklore of North American Wildflowers*, Houghton Mifflin, Boston.

Courtenay, Booth, and James H. Zimmerman, 1972. *Wildflowers and Weeds*, Van Nostrand Reinhold Company, New York.

Culpeper, Nicholas, 1990. *Culpeper's Complete Herbal & English Physician*, Meyerbooks, Glenwood, Illinois. (Reprint of 1814 London edition of *Culpeper's Complete Herbal*, originally published in London in 1652.)

Dana, Mrs. William Starr, 1893. *How to Know the Wild Flowers*, Charles Scribner's Sons, New York.

Edsall, Marian, 1985. *Roadside Plants and Flowers*, University of Wisconsin Press, Madison, Wisconsin.

Eifert, Virginia S., 1989. *Journeys in Green Places*, William Caxton Ltd., Sister Bay, Wisconsin. (Originally published by Dodd, Mead & Company, New York, 1963.)

Elias, Thomas S. and Peter A. Dykeman, 1990. *Edible Wild Plants*, Sterling Publishing Company, New York.

Fassett, Norman C., 1976. *Spring Flora of Wisconsin*, The University of Wisconsin Press, Madison, Wisconsin.

Fielder, Mildred, 1975. *Plant Medicine and Folklore*, Winchester Press, New York.

Gerard, John, *The Herball or General Historie of Plantes* (see Woodward).

Good, Mary B., 1990. *Trillium: a Guide to the Common Wildflowers of Northeastern Wisconsin*, A Horta Publication, Woodruff, Wisconsin.

Gray's Manual of Botany-A Handbook of the Flowering Plants and Ferns of the Central and North Eastern U.S. and Adjacent Canada, Eighth Edition, 1950. American Book Company, New York.

Grieve, Mrs. M., 1971. *A Modern Herbal*, Dover Publications, Inc., New York. (Originally published by Harcourt, Brace & Company, 1931.)

Jaeger, Edmund C., 1955. *A Source-Book of Biological Names and Terms*, Charles C. Thomas, Springfield, Illinois.

Keenan, Philip E., 1998. *Wild Orchids Across America*, Timber Press, Portland, Oregon.

Kieran, John, 1945. *Introduction to Wild Flowers*, Hanover House, Garden City, New York.

Klimas, John E. and James A. Cunningham, 1974. *Wildflowers of Eastern America*, Alfred A. Knopf, New York.

Korkel, Torling, 1973. *Wild Plants in Flower: The Boreal Forest and Borders*, published by Torkel Korling, Dundee, Illinois.

Korkel, Torling, 1977. *Wild Plants in Flower: Eastern Deciduous Forest*, published by Torkel Korling, Evanston, Illinois.

Luer, Carlyle, 1975. *The Native Orchids of the United States and Canada Excluding Florida*, New York Botanical Garden, New York.

Malberg, Paul and Marilyn Mahlberg, 2001. *Wildflowers of Door County*, Indiana University Press, Bloomington, Indiana.

Martin, Laura C., 1984. *Wildflower Folklore*, Fast & McMillan Publishers, Inc., Charlotte, North Carolina.

Mellinger, Marie, n.d. *Wildflowers: Ferns and Grasses of the Mountain*, The Mountain Retreat and Learning Center, Inc., Highlands, North Carolina.

Meyer, Joseph E., 1971. *The Herbalist*, Copyright by Clarence Meyer, printed in U.S.A. (Original edition printed in 1918.)

Naegele, Thomas A., 1996. *Edible and Medicinal Plants of the Great Lakes Region*, Wilderness Adventure Books, Davisburg, Michigan.

Nass, Ruby A. Kingston, 1979. *Wild Plants of Northeastern Wisconsin*, Mary Morgan, Inc., Green Bay, Wisconsin.

Neal, Bill, 1992. *Gardener's Latin*, Algonquin Books, Chapel Hill, North Carolina.

Newcomb, Lawrence, 1977. *Newcomb's Wildflower Guide*, Little, Brown & Company, Boston.

Niering, William A. and Nancy C. Olmstead, 1989. *The Audubon Society Field Guide to North American Wildflowers*, Alfred A. Knopf, Inc., New York.

Oslund, Clayton and Michele Oslund, 2001. *What's Doin' the Bloomin'?*, Plant Pics, Duluth, Minnesota.

Petrides, George A., 1958. *A Field Guide to Trees and Shrubs*, Houghton Mifflin Company, Boston.

Peterson, Lee, 1977. *Field Guide To Edible Wild Plants of Eastern/Central America*, Houghton Mifflin Company, New York.

Ranson, Nancy Richey, 1989. *Wildflowers: Legends, Poems, and Paintings*, Heard Museum Publication, McKinney, Texas.

Redington, Charles B., 1994. *Plants in Wetlands*, Kendall Hunt Publishing Company, Dubuque, Iowa.

Rickett, Harold W., 1966. *Wild Flowers of the United States, Volume 1, The Northeastern States,* McGraw-Hill Book Company, New York.

Runkel, Sylvan T. and Alvin F. Bull, 1979. *Wildflowers of Iowa Woodlands*, Wallace Homestead Book Company, Des Moines, Iowa.

Ryden, Hope, 2001. *Wildflowers Around the Year*, Clarion Books, New York.

Sander, Susan M., 1985. *Wild Flowers, A Guide for Washington Island and Door County, Wisconsin*, Susan M. Sander, Rt. 2, Box 356, Comfort TX, 78013.

Sanders, Jack, 1993. *Hedgemaids and Fairy Candles*, Ragged Mountain Press, Camden Mountain, Maine.

Schinkel, Dick, 1994. *Favorite Wildflowers of the Great Lakes and Northeastern U.S.*, Thunder Bay Press, Holt, Michigan.

Stiefel, Janice, *Selected Eastern U.S. Butterflies & Moths and Their Plant Requirements*, unpublished document.

Stokes, Donald W., 1989. *The Natural History of Wild Shrubs and Vines*, The Globe Pequot Press, Chester, Connecticut.

Tekiela, Stan, 2000. *Wild Flowers of Wisconsin Field Guide*, Adventure Publications, Inc., Cambridge, Minnesota.

The Columbia Encyclopedia, 2000. Columbia University Press, New York

Trick, Joel A., 1983. Preliminary Report on the Vascular Flora of the

Ridges Sanctuary, Baileys Harbor, Wisconsin, unpublished report to the Ridges Sanctuary.

Wells, Diana, 1997. *100 Flowers and How They Got Their Names,* Algonquin Books, Chapel Hill, North Carolina.

White, Peter, 1996. *Wildflowers of the Smokies,* Great Smokey Mountains Natural History Association, Gatlinburg, Tennessee.

Woodward, Marcus, 1964. *Gerard's Herball, The Essence Thereof Distilled by Marcus Woodward,* Spring Books, London.

Web Sites

Carter, Raphael, www.chaparraltree.com

Hebda, Richard, Royal British Columbia Museum, http://rbcm1.rbcm.gov.bc.ca/nh_papers/nativeplants

Illinois Department of Natural Resources, Illinois Natural History Survey, www.inhs.uiuc.edu/

Lacey, Laurie, www.wildworldofplants.com

Lakehead University, Faculty of Forestry and the Forest Environment, www.borealforest.org

Minnesota Department of Natural Resources, www.dnr.state.mn.us

Northern Prairie Wildlife Research Center, www.npwrc.usgs.gov

Ohio Department of Natural Resources, www.dnr.state.oh.us

Rook, Earl J. S., 1998, www.rook.org

The Nature Conservancy, www.nature.org

University of Wisconsin, Madison, Department of Botany, www.botany.wisc.edu

Wisconsin Department of Natural Resources, www.dnr.state.wi.us/org

Wisconsin State Herbarium, www.wiscinfo.doit.wisc.edu/herbarium

www.larkspurbooks.com

www.herbmed.org

Index

Achillea millefolium, 74
Actaea pachypoda, 27
Actaea rubra, 27
Agalinis purpurea, 92
Anaphalis margaritacea, 84
Andromeda glaucophylla, 29
Anemone,
   Canada, 46
   Wood, 14
Anemone acutiloba, 2
Anemone americana, 2
Anemone canadensis, 46
Anemone quinquefolia, 14
Antennaria neglecta, 9
Aquilegia canadensis, 53
Arabis lyrata, 5
Aralia nudicaulis, 40
Aralia racemosa, 56
Arbutus, Trailing, 1
Arctic Primrose, 16
Arctostaphylos uva-ursi, 20
Argentina anserina, 33
Arisaema triphyllum, 23
Asclepias incarnata, 79
Asclepias syriaca, 78
Aster,
   Calico, 94
   Large-Leaf, 94
   New England, 95
Aster lateriflorus, 94
Aster macrophyllus, 94
Aster novae-angliae, 95
Avens, Purple, 48
Baneberry,
   Red, 27
   White, 27
Bastard Toadflax, 31
Bearberry, 20
Bee Balm, 86
Beechdrops, 96
Bellwort, 12
Bergamot, Wild, 86
Big White Trillium, 15
Black-Eyed Susan, 71
Bloodroot, 3
Blue Cohosh, 24
Blue Flag, 54
Blue-Eyed Grass, 55
Bog Rosemary, 29
Broad-Leaved Toothwort, 11
Buckbean, 32
Buffaloberry, Canada, 6
Bulb-Bearing Water Hemlock, 76
Bunchberry, 35
Buttercup, Swamp, 37
Calico Aster, 94
Calopogon tuberosus, 67
Caltha palustris, 4
Camas, Death, 73
Campanula rotundifolia, 69
Canada Anemone, 46
Canada Buffaloberry, 6
Canada Goldenrod, 91
Canada Mayflower, 26
Cancer Root, 30
Cardamine concatenata, 11
Cardamine diphylla, 11
Castilleja coccinea, 25
Caulopyllum thalictroides, 24
Chelone glabra, 93
Chicory, 75
Cichorium intybus, 75
Cicuta bulbifera, 76
Circaea alpina, 50
Claytonia virginica, 10
Clintonia borealis, 36
Clintonia, 36
Cohosh, Blue, 24
Columbine, Wild, 53
Comandra umbellata, 31
Common Evening Primrose, 77
Common Milkweed, 78
Common Mullein, 72
Coptis trifolia, 21

107

Corallorhiza striata, 39
Coralroot, Striped, 39
Coreopsis lanceolata, 57
Coreopsis, Lance-Leaved, 57
Cornus canadensis, 35
Cornus stolonifera, 52
Cranberry, Highbush, 62
Cut-Leaved Toothwort, 11
Cypripedim acaule, 44
Cypripedium arietinum, 43
Cypripedium calceolus, var. *pubescens*, 44
Cypripedium reginae, 45
Death Camas, 73
Dicentra canadensis, 13
Dicentra cucullaria, 13
Dogwood, Red Osier, 52
Drosera rotundifolia, 59
Dune Goldenrod, 90
Dutchman's Breeches, 13
Dwarf Enchanter's Nightshade, 50
Dwarf Lake Iris, 17
"Endangered," 16
Epifagus virginiana, 96
Epigaea repens, 1
Epilobium angustifolium, 66
Erythronium americanum, 7
Eupatorium maculatum, 83

Evening Primrose, Common, 77
Fireweed, 66
Flower Facts:
  Annual/Biennial/Perennial, 92
  Ant Farming, 14
  Beauty of Berries, 36
  Carolus Linnaeus, 47, 71
  Doctrine of Signatures, 12
  Early Blooming Plants, 10
  Evergreens, 64
  Folk Remedies, 34
  Gaps in the Forest Canopy, 82
  Identifying Wildflowers, 65
  Introduced Plants, 75
  Invasives, 52
  Orchids, 67
  Peter Kalm, 81
  Plants Can Hurt You, 37
  Plants in Trouble, 16
  Plants That Feed off Other Plants, 30
  Reasons Not to Pick Wildflowers, 19
  Warm Days in Mid-Winter, 63
  What Is a Wildflower, 57
Fragaria virginiana, 22
Fringed Gentian, Lesser, 97
Gaultheria procumbens, 88
Gaywings, 19

Gentian,
  Lesser Fringed, 97
  Spurred, 82
Gentianopsis procera, 97
Gerardia, Purple, 92
Geum rivale, 48
Goldenrod,
  Canada, 91
  Dune, 90
  Ohio, 90
Goldthread, 21
Grass of Parnassus, 89
Grass Pink, 67
Green-Flowered Pyrola, 64
Halenia deflexa, 82
Harebell, 69
Heal-All, 68
Hepatica,
  Round-Lobed, 2
  Sharp-Lobed, 2
Highbush Cranberry, 62
Hypericum kalmianum, 80
Impatiens capensis, 85
Indian Paintbrush, 25
Indian Pipe, 61
Iris,
  Dwarf Lake, 17
  Blue Flag, 54
Iris lacustris, 17
Iris versicolor, 54
Jack-in-the-Pulpit, 23
Jewelweed, 85
Joe Pye Weed, 83
Kalm's Lobelia, 81
Kalm's St. Johnswort, 80
Kinnikinnick, 20
Labrador Tea, 38
Lady's Slipper Orchids, 42
  Pink Moccasin, 44

Ram's Head, 43
Showy, 45
Yellow, 44
Ladies Tresses, Nodding, 87
Lance-Leaved Coreopsis, 57
Large-Leaf Aster, 94
Ledum groenlandicum, 38
Lesser Fringed Gentian, 97
Lilium philadelphicum, 70
Lily,
Blue Bead, 36
Trout, 7
Wood, 70
Linnaea borealis, 47
Lobelia kalmii, 81
Lobelia, Kalm's, 81
Long-Spurred Violet, 8
Loosestrife, Tufted, 60
Lyre-Leaved Rock Cress, 5
Lysimachia thyrsiflora, 60
Maianthemum canadense, 26
Marsh Marigold, 4
Mayflower, Canada, 26
Menyanthes trifoliata, 32
Milkweed,
Common, 78
Swamp, 79
Monarda fistulosa, 86
Moneses uniflora, 63
Monotropa uniflora, 61
Mullein, Common, 72

New England Aster, 95
Nightshade, Dwarf Enchanter's, 50
Nodding Ladies Tresses, 87
Nuphar variegata, 41
Oenothera biennis, 77
Ohio Goldenrod, 90
Orobanche uniflora, 30
Osmorhiza claytonii, 34
Parnassia glauca, 89
Pearly Everlasting, 84
Pink Moccasin Lady's Slipper, 44
Pink-Flowered Pyrola, 65
Pitcher Plant, 49
Polygala paucifolia, 19
Pond Lily, Yellow, 41
Primrose, Arctic, 16
Primula mistassinica, 16
Prunella vulgaris, 68
Purple Avens, 48
Purple Gerardia, 92
Pussytoes, 9
Pyrola,
Green-Flowered, 64
Pink-Flowered, 65
Pyrola asarifolia, 65
Pyrola chlorantha, 64
Ram's Head Lady's Slipper, 43
Ranunculus hispidus, 37
Red Baneberry, 27
Red Osier Dogwood, 52
Rock Cress, Lyre-Leaved, 5
Rosa blanda, 51
Rose, Wild, 51

Round-Leaved Sundew, 59
Round-Lobed Hepatica, 2
Rubus parviflorus, 58
Rudbeckia hirta, 71
Sanguinaria canadensis, 3
Sarracenia purpurea, 49
Sarsaparilla, Wild, 40
Self-Heal, 68
Sharp-Lobed Hepatica, 2
Shepherdia canadensis, 6
Shinleaf
Greenish-Flowered, 64
One-Flowered, 63
Pink, 65
Showy Lady's Slipper, 45
Shrubby St. Johnswort, 80
Silverweed, 33
Sisyrinchium montanum, 55
Sium suave, 76
Smilicina stellata, 28
Solidago canadensis, 91
Solidago ohioensis, 90
Solidago simplex var. *gillmanii*, 90
"Special Concern," 16
Spikenard, 56
Spiranthes cernua, 87
Spring Beauty, 10
Spurred Gentian, 82
Squirrel Corn, 13
St. Johnswort, Kalm's, 80
St. Johnswort, Shrubby, 80

Starflower, 18
Starry False Solomon's Seal, 28
Starry Solomon's Plume, 28
Strawberry, Wild, 22
Striped Coralroot, 39
Sundew, Round-Leaved, 59
Swamp Buttercup, 37
Swamp Milkweed, 79
Sweet Cicely, 34
Thimbleberry, 58
"Threatened," 16
Toadflax, Bastard, 31
Toothwort
  Broad-Leaved, 11
  Cut-Leaved, 11
Touch-Me Not, 85
Trailing Arbutus, 1
Trientalis borealis, 18
Trillium grandiflorum, 15
Trillium, Big White, 15
Trout Lily, 7
Tufted Loosestrife, 60
Turtlehead, 93
Twinflower, 47
Uvularia grandiflora, 12
Verbascum thapsus, 72
Viburnum opulus, subsp. *trilobum*, 62
Viola rostrata, 8
Violet, Long-Spurred, 8
Water Hemlock, Bulb-Bearing, 76
Water Parsnip, 76
White Baneberry, 27
Wild Bergamot, 86
Wild Columbine, 53
Wild Rose, 51
Wild Sarsaparilla, 40
Wild Strawberry, 22
Wintergreen, 88
Wood Anemone, 14
Wood Lily, 70
Wood Nymph, 63
Yarrow, 74
Yellow Lady's Slipper, 44
Yellow Pond Lily, 41
Zigadenus elegans, 73

✓ — June 12, 2003

Checklist of Wildflowers of the Ridges Sanctuary and Logan Creek

Date Seen	Flower Name
_____	Arctic Primrose
✓	Bastard Toadflax
✓	Bearberry
_____	Beechdrops
✓	Bellwort
✓	Big White Trillium
_____	Black-Eyed Susan
_____	Bloodroot
_____	Blue Cohosh
_____	Blue Flag
_____	Blue-Eyed Grass
_____	Bog Rosemary
_____	Broad-Leaved Toothwort
✓	Buckbean
✓	Bulb-Bearing Water Hemlock
_____	Bunchberry
_____	Calico Aster
_____	Canada Anemone
_____	Canada Buffaloberry
✓	Canada Goldenrod
✓	Canada Mayflower
_____	Cancer Root
✓	Chicory
✓	Clintonia

Date Seen	Flower Name
_____	Common Evening Primrose
_____	Common Milkweed
_____	Common Mullein
_____	Cut-Leaved Toothwort
_____	Death Camas
_____	Dune Goldenrod
_____	Dutchman's Breeches
_____	Dwarf Enchanter's Nightshade
✓	Dwarf Lake Iris
✓	Fireweed
✓	Gaywings
_____	Goldthread
_____	Grass of Parnassus
_____	Grass Pink
_____	Green-Flowered Pyrola
_____	Harebell
✓	Highbush Cranberry
✓	Indian Paintbrush
_____	Indian Pipe
_____	Jack-in-the-Pulpit
_____	Jewelweed
_____	Joe Pye Weed
_____	Kalm's Lobelia

Date Seen	Flower Name	Date Seen	Flower Name
___	Kalm's St. Johnswort	___	Spring Beauty
✓	Labrador Tea	___	Spurred Gentian
___	Lance-Leaved Coreopsis	✓	Starflower
___	Large-Leaf Aster	___	Starry Solomon's Plume
___	Lesser Fringed Gentian	✓	Striped Coralroot
___	Long-Spurred Violet	✓	Swamp Buttercup
___	Lyre-Leaved Rock Cress	___	Swamp Milkweed
✓	Marsh Marigold	___	Sweet Cicely
___	New England Aster	___	Thimbleberry
___	Nodding Ladies Tresses	___	Touch-Me-Not
___	Ohio Goldenrod	___	Trailing Arbutus
___	Pearly Everlasting	___	Trout Lily
___	Pink Moccasin Lady's Slipper	___	Tufted Loosestrife
___	Pink-Flowered Pyrola	___	Turtlehead
___	Pitcher Plant	___	Twinflower
___	Purple Avens	___	White Baneberry
___	Purple Gerardia	___	Wild Bergamot
___	Pussytoes	✓	Wild Columbine
✓	Ram's Head Lady's Slipper	___	Wild Rose
___	Red Baneberry	✓	Wild Sarsaparilla
___	Red Osier Dogwood	✓	Wild Strawberry
___	Round-Leaved Sundew	___	Wintergreen
___	Round-Lobed Hepatica	___	Wood Anemone
___	Self-Heal	___	Wood Lily
___	Sharp-Lobed Hepatica	___	Wood Nymph
___	Showy Lady's Slipper	___	Yarrow
___	Silverweed	✓	Yellow Lady's Slipper
___	Spikenard	___	Yellow Pond Lily